F*CK THE GLASS CEILING

F*CK THE GLASS CEILING

START AT THE TOP (AND STAY THERE) AS A FEMININE ENTREPRENEUR

MANDY CAVANAUGH

F*CK THE GLASS CEILING
Start at the Top (and Stay There) as a Feminine Entrepreneur

ISBN 978-1-5445-1738-4 *Hardcover*
      978-1-5445-1736-0 *Paperback*
      978-1-5445-1737-7 *Ebook*

This book is dedicated to my mom,
Sharon L. Deats,
the IFL who made everything possible.

CONTENTS

INTRODUCTION

FAILURE TO THRIVE

"Tails."

With the flip of a coin, I decided what to study in graduate school.

Like most college graduates of the twentieth century, I came out of university with the enculturated belief that being a corporate employee under a solid brand with a clear path to advancement was the most honorable thing I could accomplish. Upon graduation, that notion landed me in a sales role for a well-known Fortune 100 consumer goods company.

From day one, I felt uncomfortable in my role. I couldn't figure out the reporting I was supposed to do and didn't want to ask my boss to explain it a third time. It wasn't just the reporting that made me uncomfortable; I had an undiagnosed autoimmune condition that masked itself as depression. Two or three days per month, I'd skip going on my ninety-store route because I couldn't get out of bed.

My actual sales results were outstanding—as I discovered only when my district manager shared them with me the day I resigned, six months into the job. This positive feedback being withheld from me turned out to be extremely pivotal in the very direction of my life. I was allergic to the feeling of failure, so I ran.

Upon consulting with my supportive soon-to-be husband and college sweetheart, we decided the best option for my future would be to go back to graduate school. But what to study? In keeping with the budding entrepreneur I would eventually become, I ran my decision through a rigorous cost-benefit analysis. In other words, I flipped a coin: heads, master of public administration; tails, master of science in healthcare administration.

So healthcare it was. And for a few extra classes, I decided to double down and earn an MBA.

Part of the requirement to earn the MS was a one-year residency, which found me working at a community hospital, where, after what I had studied for six years in college, I believed I could contribute. It quickly became evident, however, that the field of healthcare doesn't reward innovation or creativity. The focus wasn't on making people healthier; it was on getting heads in beds. And even the most talented of graduates were looking at a fifteen- to twenty-year-long path to being a hospital CEO in an industry where the executives work twice as hard for less compensation than they'd earn in a non-healthcare setting.

In true-to-form control-freak style, I lined up the timing of my first child's birth to coincide with the last week of my residency and moved back to Houston two days after he was born. At the ripe old age of twenty-five, I had a family, three degrees, and an extraordinary amount of pent-up ambition.

The first four months of my son's life were the most blissful I'd ever experienced. That is, until my favorite graduate-school professor interrupted that bliss by offering me a part-time role as the director of executive education in his consulting firm. When Dr. Dalston shared that he was collaborating with global thought leaders to train groups of hospital CEOs in the world's largest for-profit system, it was a no-brainer. My first two careers hadn't panned out, so I felt like I needed a win. Beyond being a profound boost to my résumé in the ultracompetitive world of healthcare administration—without having to run a hospital—it was a prestigious role that brought with it a certain amount of clout for whatever future role I might seek.

From the clarity of hindsight, the reality is that my drive to accomplish has been the biggest influence in my life decisions. Unfortunately for my son and me, back then, I wasn't trained to make those choices based on my feelings.

Although every moment I'd spent with him since his birth found me in a state of ecstasy, my relentless pursuit of achievement was an equally opposing force. I didn't feel free to openly share this strong internal conflict when I thought about having to choose between staying home and working. I was a child of the eighties—a time when it seemed every woman had to choose a side in the cultural battle between stay-at-home and career moms.

Despite not really wanting to take a job so soon, I heard

the word "yes" come out of my mouth while ignoring the shooting pain of sadness that ripped through my heart.

One by one, at a breakneck pace, I was checking all the boxes of success:

- ☑ Education
- ☑ Husband
- ☑ House in the suburbs
- ☑ Baby
- ☑ Job

I was on a path instilled in me by family, professors, and society that was consistent with what a twenty-something-year-old *should want to do.*

My boss and I had an agreement that I'd only work three days a week, which at first seemed harmless enough. Then came the soul-wrenching routine of taking my tiny baby to a total stranger, placing his car seat on the floor next to five other infants at 6 a.m., and making the hour-long commute to downtown Houston. Every time I handed him off, I pretended his waterfall of massive tears was okay. When I returned to the seclusion of my car every morning, the tears rolled down my own face.

Three days per week quickly turned into four. While I tried to continue breastfeeding, it was awkward as hell to pump at my desk. It was summer in Texas, and each time I locked the door and took my lactation break (at my desk), I ended up covered in sweat and milk while wearing only the bottom half of my suit. I was literally a hot mess. My supply dried up within a month, dashing my hopes to nurse until he was a year old.

It was no surprise I turned out to be a mediocre employee. I was terrible at juggling the myriad of details coordinating events across different time zones—which ironically was the exact type of work I'd later recruit and train teams to perform in my company. No matter how much I loved the idea of planning conferences, this role just didn't align with my strengths. My true calling was to *lead* conferences, which is an entire galaxy away from organizing them.

The tipping point came when a London hotel booked my boss into the same room as a female client, and I hadn't caught it. Although my boss forgave me for this and another big mishap, I couldn't forgive myself. I felt like a failure at fitting the corporate mold...again.

Then, in the course of a single weekend, everything changed.

BEHIND THE MASK

"F*ck you and the horse you rode in on?" I submitted.

I was at the front of the class, looking at a close-up of my face displayed on a large TV screen. The seminar leader had asked me to say what I saw in the image, which had been filmed earlier with an instruction to "relax my face and let down my social mask."

One of my coworkers, an industrial psychologist and professional coach, had observed my inner turmoil and recommended I attend a weekend business workshop to experience a method for finding my true calling based on *what lights me up.*

One of the steps in that method was for the leader, along with the group, to take a reading of your face with zero facial expression on it. They also showed photos of babies' faces so you could see what happens to our "lights" as we get older. The feedback we received about signals captured in the images (as well as our breathing, etc.) helped reorganize one's consciousness in a way that cannot be easily explained—but it still woke me up.

On its own, the idea that if you choose a career that brings joyful aliveness to your being, the money will follow was not so revolutionary. After all, it was the mid-nineties, and the personal development industry's "follow your bliss" movement was trending. But Sage University, the pioneers of this method, rocked my world with the experience of being observed *with curiosity* and *without opinion*. Their seminar curriculum centered around recognizing a participant's energy level based on questions that confronted their innate genius, which, for most people, had been unobserved due to the suppression of natural powers of observation during childhood.

The most surprising, clearest feedback I received from my coaches was that, based on what caused me to light up the most, my true function was "telling people what to do."

Seriously? At first, I was embarrassed. But as I looked around the room, the whole group was beaming with what looked like profound appreciation. My body took in a deeply relaxing, parasympathetic breath.

In that moment, I was awakened to a pearl of innate wisdom I'd been hiding from myself. I knew that if I allowed myself to embody this new information and let it unfold, it would play a pivotal role in my future.

"You're supposed to be your own boss. And everyone else's as well," the seminar leader informed me with a belly laugh.

What a relief! I can follow my function by leading people who want to be led. Maybe now I could learn to embrace that bossy little girl who lived inside me—the one who tried so hard to "be friendly and fit in" while wanting to f*ck up the status quo wherever she went. Maybe I could show her to the door, let her out, and let her fully step into her purpose. *Maybe she could be loved for who she really is.*

THIRD TIME'S A CHARM

Even though I had just launched my second career, I immediately went home after the seminar and fervently shared with my husband how I wanted to start a business. Not tomorrow. Not someday. *Now.*

What I did next, and the speed at which I did it, I don't necessarily recommend doing. The following Monday—much to the chagrin of my boss—I quit my job. (In case you're seeing a pattern—yes, my decisiveness has proven to be a problem at times.)

But after that class, I was so inspired and fired up, and as I'd mentioned, I wasn't exactly a genius at coordinating international seminars. The cherry on top of the new plan was that I'd no longer have to choose between having a career and being with my son. My new coaches had shown me how to see a business *as a family system*. (I took these instructions to heart, and I'm going to show you how I did it.)

Over the following weeks, I began talking to everyone who'd listen to me about my intent to be an entrepreneur. I decided to focus on real estate development and commercial property management because those were the industries I'd been the most curious about. These businesses also lined up with my desire for my new calling to be lucrative, because I highly value financial freedom. Knowing I couldn't have my son driving around to appointments with me as a real estate agent, I had to find another specialty. Although I didn't yet know what that path would be, I was led to the idea that I needed to seek out conversations with the most successful professionals I could find among friends and family.

One conversation led to another until I heard the Army was seeking companies to manage barracks at a nearby base. I called an Army friend and asked what he thought about me trying to start a company to win that business. And guess what?

In a moment of synchronicity, at the time of my phone call, this friend just happened to be seeking remote housing solutions for his troops.

He told me, "I need someone to set up apartments with furniture, linens, pots, pans, and toothbrush holders in a few remote towns around the United States where barracks don't exist. Do you think you're qualified to do that?"

"Of course!" I exclaimed, knowing in my gut it was the absolute truth.

After some negotiation and collaboration, my husband and I formed a partnership in which I ran the company while he continued working at his job and handling our startup's small amount of accounting in the evenings. I cleared out my living and dining rooms, had a business phone line installed, and bought a desk, a laptop, and a fax machine. I put a twin-sized mattress on the floor for my son to play on and added a small jungle gym I'd bought at a garage sale.

After a steep learning curve, some humbling mistakes, maxing out every credit card we could get our hands on, and a lot of long days juggling my child, my client, suppliers, lawyers, CPAs, and the like—I had three projects in three states. I was having a blast. What I didn't realize at that super-intense phase of the business launch was that in precisely the same week I'd started the business, I'd also become pregnant...*with twins*.

Of course, the news made me feel like I'd won the lottery, but looking back, I would have been completely justified to try to shut down the company. Fortunately for my future self, there was no going back. I was already under contract with the US government, in addition to courting two large defense contractors who were now expressing an interest in working with us. I didn't realize it at the time, but creating *point-of-no-return* circumstances would become one of my signature CEO strategies.

When things kicked into high gear, I talked my mom into leaving her real estate firm to work with me. Then, after I gave birth to my daughters a month early, my husband took paternity leave from his employer. Weeks of nursing for literally twelve hours per day was motivation enough for me to steal him away from his employer. Besides helping change diapers all day and being the best daytime dad anyone could ask for, he held 49 percent ownership in the company, and we desperately needed his CFO and sales skills to keep the momentum. Besides, we had finally started turning a profit during the sixth month in business, and the company could now afford to pay us both. The rest is history, as they say.

WHY I WROTE THIS

The information you hold in your hands isn't meant to be a masterpiece—it's designed to be a resource for you as a feminine figure who is doing one of the most courageous things you can do—starting and running your own company. My highest choice isn't to win accolades but to alleviate suffering.

You might have guessed from the title of the book I'm not one to comply with societal norms. Still, why on earth would I write a book geared specifically toward *feminine* leaders? Isn't focusing on gender politically incorrect? Isn't it so *last century*? Trust me, the whole concept of "feminine" leadership was the farthest thing from my mind during my first dozen years in business. Until, upon a request from the mentor and colleague who'd helped me pivot into my entrepreneurial life, I played the role of facilitator at Global Women's Entrepreneurship Conferences in Spain and the United States.

It wasn't until speaking in the front of these rooms full of women that I discovered the chasm that exists between ultracompetitive, classically trained female leaders (who can embody either masculine or feminine energy on demand but are also few and far between outside of corporate jobs) and the struggles that more inexperienced and/or strictly *feminine* entrepreneurs were having.

As a side gig to keep my coaching tools sharpened, I then trained entrepreneurs at a few other seminars, and they all illuminated *the same challenges*. Challenges such as confidence, conflict resolution, working closely with alpha men, building and leading teams, and juggling one's personal life with owning a business. Most of them were starving for a perspective different from the classic masculine-modeled version of being at the top of an organization (or even being part of an organization, for many of them).

There was only one problem. The versions of leadership I had learned and embodied up to that point, which had been designed from a masculine perspective and carried out over hundreds of years, would never work for most of the budding feminine entrepreneurs who showed up in my classes. Why? *Because the percentage of females who want to take the pressure of a C-level job is a fraction of the percentage of males who are willing to take it.* I'll go into this phenomenon in detail in chapter 1, share why it matters, and spend the rest of the book illuminating what to do about it.

Each occurrence of these women asking me for coaching presented me with a double bind because I hadn't even thought about how to run a business and preserve my innate feminine essence. Taking pressure, and even creating it, was my comfort zone.

But my passion for recognizing, developing, and training leaders was oozing from the core of my being, as my brilliant mentor had recognized. So I would have fun with my seminar participants by playing with their feminine nature and bending it to my entrepreneurship methods. The results were astounding, as we healed each other's confidence and created new stories about what's possible in leadership. These stories informed my collaborations with colleagues and clients for years to come, leading to wildly greater success and satisfaction. Thus, a new mission was born.

THE MISSION

If I had to sum up my purpose in one sentence, it would be this: I'd like to have millions more feminine leaders become successful, putting them in positions to substantively change how governments, corporations, and communities are led by bringing new perspectives to persistent problems. I'll expand more on those persistent problems later while entertaining you with some data. In the meantime, and most importantly, what I want for you is to be the most powerful, relaxed, satisfied leader you can be.

After the publication of a 1943 seminal paper entitled "A Theory of Human Motivation," American psychologist Abraham Maslow became known for one of modern psychology's most iconic motivational theories, the hierarchy of needs. Depicted as a pyramid with self-actualization at the top, the hierarchy of needs describes the phases that human motivation generally includes on the path toward realizing one's fullest potential.

Starting at the bottom of the pyramid with one's most basic

needs, the first is "physiological" (air, water, food, shelter, sleep, clothing, reproduction), followed by the second, "safety" (personal security, employment, resources, health, property). Further up the hierarchy, when one has successfully taken care of their basic survival needs, they then have the bandwidth to pursue "love and belonging" (friendship, intimacy, family, sense of connection). The fourth level on the hierarchy is "esteem" (respect, self-esteem, status, recognition, strength, freedom), and the final level is "self-actualization" (becoming the most that one can be).[1]

While this hierarchy is still often referred to in business and taught in universities, the parts of Maslow's work most relevant to you and me being happy have been largely ignored. First, although he deployed a pyramid in his reference to human needs, Maslow's writings never actually referred to a hierarchy.[2] Instead, he emphasized that the state of being called "self-actualization" requires one to *transcend* his or her basic needs to integrate into a creative, purpose-driven life.

In other words, when it comes to self-actualization, the *means is the end.*

Fortunately, I've practiced this little-known distinction from Maslow's theories for more than two decades, and I can report that, as a CEO, you *can* and *should* use it to your advantage. Therefore, this book is full of adaptable, proven practices on how to do just that.

I've met modern CEOs, from US technology firms to Andean farming co-ops, who also recognize that maximizing human potential is the path to creating fully engaged employees and sustainable economies that lift people out of poverty while tying their livelihoods to that bigger purpose.

These contemporary chief executives understand that humanity is more likely to create unprecedented outcomes when connected to a higher purpose. For this reason, and because newer generations of workers seek deeper meaning in their jobs, an increasing number of firms newly measure things such as a double bottom line, which includes both financial performance and social impact. This, in turn, contributes to the feeling of being self-actualized among the stakeholders.

When I first became an entrepreneur and coach, the majority of CEOs I associated with viewed financial success and doing what inspires you as disparate ideas rather than two aspects of a single career. The proliferation of the more modern notion of success is why business coaching has increased to an industry worth more than $10 billion annually.

Still, if you take a glance at the content of the more shallow "CEO mindset" influencers online, you'll get the impression that living a purpose-driven life is correlated with the pursuit of money, power, and material things. Don't get me wrong—I'd be lying if I said I don't love driving fast cars in Emilio Pucci heels. But what you as a discerning entrepreneur surely recognize by now is that going after material things is not the path but a potential *by-product* of transcending the need to have material items to feel alive.

What I've seen countless times, and also painfully experienced, is that if someone places money, adoration, and power before being in service (to one's employees or clients, for example), one's ego is going to land him or her in the middle of an addictive loop. In other words, if prestige and material comfort are all that motivate you, you'll never have enough, and that's going to leave within you a near-constant emptiness—no matter what you do or purchase.

While you might engage in dopamine-seeking behaviors, they won't satiate you. They might provide you with temporary enjoyment, but they won't give you an *experience* of play, because pressure and self-absorption make you unable to relax. Maybe this is why so many millionaires, celebrities, rock stars, and politicians—when removed from their sphere of power and influence—turn out to have disastrously drama-filled *real lives*.

Successful entrepreneurs understand that a business will become a catalyst for bringing to the surface any psychological, spiritual, or even physical problems we may need to heal. When these issues are seen at play, they present an opportunity to heal and ascend beyond them. Of course, it's easier said than done. But I will assure you that if you can change your mindset to understand that challenges happen *for* you and not just *to* you—these challenges can provide unique opportunities for growth and can add up to you overcoming a limited mindset. This is the phenomenon I love most about playing the business game.

My business became a catalyst for psychological and spiritual growth that no other aspect of my life could have. In addition to running my businesses as a path toward that growth, I've invested a vast amount of time and money immersing myself in executive roundtables and mastery groups and been fortunate enough to collaborate and provide consulting to solopreneurs, middle-market companies—all the way to companies of one hundred thousand employees. To take things as far as I could on this path of development, I also earned coaching certifications in high-performance leadership, entrepreneurship, conscious language, and outcome facilitation.

Since it's just you and me chatting here, I'll be honest and tell you that I thought about quitting *at least* 487 times, but once I figured out how to build a sustainable system that supported me in doing exactly what I wanted to do and nothing more, my quitting urges ceased. By reading this book and playing the business game the way I teach it, you'll learn how to organize around being in service, all the while organizing *your business around serving you.*

All good CEOs are in constant learning mode, myself included. And most veteran entrepreneurs know that CEO-ship in the trenches is an entirely different beast than studying it in a university, taking online classes, or gaining experience as an employee. Preparing for the big game is just that—preparation. None of the theory matters until you step onto the field because that's how you learn—through trial, error, taking hits, and getting back up. Thus, my goal is to help you achieve a deeper level of mastery in running a successful business rather than some passive academic theory you might learn in college—because, last time I checked, most business colleges are preparing students to work for someone else.

On the following pages, when I share information about leading teams, providing jobs, creating wealth, and raising kids—all while experiencing heartbreak, health issues, and economic setbacks—I'm stating that you can have challenges *and* be a wildly successful entrepreneur. In fact, let's *assume* that you'll have difficulties, and some of them may seem impossible to overcome.

When you learn that you are mostly playing against yourself, you're no longer bothered by the competition. You gain a deeper understanding that there are no enemies, only opponents. You learn to "tune into the playing field" rather than see what other people want you to see. Most importantly, you learn to be present to what is happening right now—in the present moment—what you can do about it, and how it will impact your results in the long run.

It surprises some entrepreneurs that if you're a business owner, you're also the chief executive, and the day you start your company is the time to start acting like one. (The only exception is if you immediately hire someone to replace you at the top—which is expensive and also not a good idea at the beginning.) To act like a CEO, you must *think* like one. Fortunately, while you'll soon learn that I have many shortcomings, teaching women CEO-ship is one of my strong suits.

Although there are many paths up the mountain of growing a thriving business, the ideas herein are presented through the prism of my experiences, courses, coaching tools, books, and decades of executive roundtables and mentors that have influenced my thinking. Whether you're running a technology company that deploys millions in capital or presiding over a coffee shop with three employees, a majority of the same principles apply.

In sharing with you the same teachings I've seen most appreciated by the women I've coached and teams I've led, I want to give you insights to implement your highest vision for growing your company and your wealth while keeping your balance. I'm also going to lay out some of the pitfalls I've experienced throughout several decades of business leadership, with the hopes that you can avoid at least some of them.

With that said, if you're not yet an entrepreneur, and the main thing you get out of this book is greater appreciation for your job (and respect for the founder of the company where you work), then that's a great accomplishment too! Regardless of what happens, I intend to help you bring peace of mind to knowing you're on *your* right path. If working for a great organization sounds more appealing after you put this book down, the information can still be valuable to you. Why? Because if you want to get promoted, especially to top leadership, you need to think like an owner. And if your career doesn't currently offer the opportunities to implement any of these ideas, well, you might get inspired to find one that does.

DIVINE FEMININE ENERGY

As I alluded to in the section explaining why I wrote this book, I feel that humanity is being called to restore *divine feminine energy* to leadership at all levels. And as I've also insinuated, that begins with you. I know I should probably address the question you might be asking: What does "restoring divine feminine energy" mean?

Before I explain, I want to lay out a vitally important distinction I'll use throughout this book.

- When I use the words *feminine* and *masculine*, I'm referring to *energies that any individual can embody* to varying degrees.
- When I use the words *female* or *male*, I am referring to *gender*.

In this book, I'm speaking to a primarily female audience but would love nothing more than for every male leader on planet Earth to be able to access his own feminine energy on demand. (I also try hard to teach feminine entrepreneurs to be able to view things through a masculine perspective, to the extent I am able.)

None of my generalizations are intended to offend or stereotype in harmful ways. That said, I would like to issue my disclaimer at the outset: there are politically incorrect and potentially controversial statements in the book—none of which are meant to be a dogma or decree. A cursory look at masculine and feminine traits applied to a normal distribution curve shows that a very small portion of males will be more feminine than the majority of females, and a small number of females will be more masculine than the majority of men.[3]

Besides influencing our physical bodies, the hormones of being male or female influence our brains, and when analyzed as a group, there is a 30 percent overlap between each gender on masculine and feminine traits. To me, this is significant enough to assert that there are significant differences between the average female and average male, whether biological or environmental, in the expression of the energies of feminine and masculine.

Many cultures have ways of explaining feminine and masculine energies, including references to yin and yang, Shiva and Shakti, and so forth. When I refer to the phrase "divine feminine energy" I am referring to the purest blueprint of feminine essence within the universe, which contributes equally to everything that is manifested. So when I say that we should restore divine feminine energy to all levels of leadership, I am suggesting that feminine figures assume their power and collaborate with masculine figures in power and that each of us (women and men) also have that balance within ourselves.

In my personal experience, modern society has cultivated women to draw upon their innate masculine energy to such a degree that gaps have been created in our family systems in the same way the world at large has been damaged by the same imbalance. I am not putting the onus on women as being the cause of this trend, nor am I placing it on men, particularly. Rather, I am focusing on *moving forward with solutions* that benefit us all.

With that said, I intend to show you how *being feminine* has been highly underrated in leadership and how to overcome it. Women are ingrained with a biological skillset that concerns us with wholeness, compassion, and connection, as opposed to the masculine imperative, which is to conquer, control, and compete.[4] In my observation, women are more likely to be empathic and to see things more holistically, with less risk of over-compartmentalizing their decisions, which leads to fewer unintended consequences.

When you recognize these traits as inherent leadership strengths (rather than weaknesses, as outdated societal programming might dictate), you'll come to find they're some of the most powerful tools in your toolbox. With the advantage of having a uniquely complex way of seeing things, you're poised to be a powerful, effective CEO who's built to lead twenty-first-century businesses. If we want to restore balance so global leadership can function optimally, that balance must begin within ourselves—as founders, idea generators, innovators, executives, and CEOs.

I'll assume throughout this book that you want to reach your potential through growing your company, building wealth, and winning at life while *preserving the majority of your feminine energy (or at least keeping it accessible)* rather than just learning how to "outman" the men you'll be working with and competing against.

When the situation or circumstance dictates, sometimes stepping into masculine energy can be both the right choice and your saving grace. But unless you have the nature to be a manly leader and enjoy embodying it, if you want to feel fulfilled in your relationships, parenting, social life, and health, it's imperative for you to be authentic to your feminine nature. (Even the lesbian leaders I know who embody masculine energy seem to remain feminine in their thinking and highly empathic in their perspective.)

Throughout this book, and especially in chapter 2, I'm going to spend a lot of time painting a picture of what I call *Inspired Feminine Leadership*. I will also lay out why it's important—besides the fact that being uninspired, bashing masculinity, and putting quotas on hiring hasn't worked out so well, which I discuss in chapter 1.

CHAPTER 1

170 YEARS LATER, FEMINISM FAILS

Before and after World War II, men would go off to work to earn a paycheck while a majority of the women stayed home or worked to support the war, stalling the women's rights movement (which had started in the 1800s and would give us the right to vote and own property) for a couple of decades. Then, in the 1960s, when birth control became available and the civil rights movement took off, we went into the workforce en masse.

We owe a massive debt of gratitude to the pioneering women who came before us, who ardently blazed a trail on which we could travel. From the first wave of suffragists who spent forty years on winning our right to vote, to the second wave of activists who weakened the stronghold of traditional role stereotypes and ushered in the idea of females having equal access to participation in all aspects of a society's way of life, I have extreme respect for the privilege of being able to flippantly suggest that a woman simply *start at the top*.

Although I don't resonate with everything she said, the

American activist and spokeswoman for the feminist movement, Gloria Steinem, once stated, "The purpose of feminism is to free the uniqueness of the individual and to understand that inside each of us is a unique human being who is a combination of heredity and environment." To me, this sounds like common sense. But at the time she said it, the notion of individualism was provocative.

A third wave of feminism picked up again in the nineties, which also positively blew me away because it finally brought consciousness to our ideas about gender, sexuality, the qualities of being masculine and feminine, and the media-driven definitions of beauty, as well as attracting more male participation.

As I write this, we are a few years into the fourth wave, which has the wind at its back due to the power of social media, where trafficking, rape culture, body shaming, marginalizing of minorities, and other forms of oppression can be brought to awareness and dismantled.

While subject matter experts and social justice professionals are better equipped to discuss what has worked and not worked within each of these movements, what's clear is that efforts for equal representation in senior leadership in corporate America, while perhaps well intentioned, have fallen desperately short.

As I raised a family and worked with these corporations as a supplier, I naively assumed that because the third wave of feminism was in full force during my college days and because these corporations were doubling down on their commitment to diversity, a new crop of feminine leaders would find themselves in the highest levels of governments and global corporations. I was wrong.

THE GLASS CEILING

Coined by management consultant Marilyn Loden in a 1978 speech, the "glass ceiling" is defined as an intangible barrier within a hierarchy that prevents women or minorities from obtaining upper-level positions. Unfortunately, this phrase is still relevant today. For decades, consultants, academics, and corporate leaders have performed studies, interviewed tens of thousands of men and women, and published findings. Social activists, political lobbies, and legislators have mounted a full-court press of proposed solutions—with limited results.

McKinsey & Company, an American management consulting firm, began publishing annual research in 2015 regarding the gaps in female representation in the senior management of US companies. According to a finding from their earliest reports, one of the main reasons for the lack of women at the top of America's corporations is that *females lose their ambition.*

Later in their research, McKinsey & Company adopted a theory called the "broken rung." The broken rung suggests that when it comes to promoting women, discrepancies and failures begin at the first level of management. In turn, this broken rung lowers the trajectory of female representation for each level, all the way up to the C-suite.[5] Hence the perception of a glass ceiling.

Chances are likely you've heard all about the glass ceiling, but have you heard the term *glass cliff*? This notion began circulating in corporate leadership circles around 2005 and is based on the fact that women are selected more frequently to lead projects, business units, and companies that are in crisis mode. Evidence for the glass cliff phenomenon has been supported by both experimental and qualitative methods, and as of the editing of this book, an online search on Forbes.com for the "glass cliff" yielded forty-two articles.

Because women are perceived as better suited to socioemotional challenges, they are viewed as the better choice for managing companies in crisis and turnaround situations. Does this seem like it would increase the pressure of a job and the intensity of one's stress? As a former turnaround consultant, I can tell you it does. What do you think it would do to a leader's overall win/loss statistics to be placed more frequently in crisis situations? And would that, perhaps, have a negative bearing on your promotability to highly viable projects in the future?

No wonder these women are falling off an invisible cliff.[6]

Before I dismantle the theories about what needs to be done to solve the glass cliff problem, let's review a short list of reasons that have been cited for the existence of women being affected by it:

1. Women are *choosing* to leave their high-powered posts.[7]
2. Women are not prepared to make the required commitment.[8]
3. Women experience detrimental pressures of family and social norms.[9]

4. Women have different ambition levels and drive.[10]
5. Women are vulnerable to aspects of the work culture, or "push" factors.[11]
6. Women are opting for family and lifestyle demands, or "pull" factors.[12]
7. Women are leaving work because their jobs are neither meaningful nor satisfying.[13]
8. Women feel undervalued and see a lack of opportunity.[14]
9. Women may receive a disproportionate share of the blame for things set in motion before they took control of disproportionately underperforming areas.[15]
10. Women feel a lack of acknowledgment of both the difficulties and accomplishment of handling the underperforming areas.[16]
11. Women feel battle-scarred and burned-out, and withdraw from the experiences of these crises.[17]
12. Women are overrepresented in vulnerable professions.[18]
13. Women have unbalanced work-life roles.[19]
14. Women have to perform increased "emotional labor" at work.[20]
15. Women are exposed to more significant stress than their male counterparts as they advance up the corporate ladder.[21]
16. Women experience increased stress, which leads to adverse effects on job performance,[22] commitment,[23] and absenteeism.[24]
17. Women become disillusioned with the organization as well as their job.[25]
18. Women disidentify with their organizations and distance themselves from them[26] through reduced motivation,[27] cooperation,[28] and commitment to decisions.[29]
19. Women feel they are less a part of the informal network of communication (aka "old schoolboys networks"),

which help provide support to cope with the difficulties in the glass-cliff roles.[30]

It's quite a list, isn't it? To overcome this multitude of reasons for female leaders departing, corporations have spent considerable effort and untold billions on programs aimed at *keeping women motivated* to promote gender diversity.

Unfortunately, motivation as a strategy to keep women engaged in crisis-laden, stressful, overburdened roles is like pouring water into a leaky bucket. Since no one has cracked the code on why the billions of dollars in programs are yielding little results, I will throw myself into the briar patch and give my opinion.

SAMENESS DOESN'T CREATE DIVERSITY

"We are conceptualizing a synergistic, seamless process for cross-functionally creating an end-to-end infrastructure solution using a minimum of human capital and leveraging technology on the back end," the buying committee member said.

WTF? I thought to myself. *Why do they have to co-opt as many words from the English language as possible in each sentence? Why not just talk normally?*

As an entrepreneur selling into huge corporations and interacting with the dynamics at their headquarters, I would often feel anxiety about being assimilated into their cultures of homogenous standardization. I know it might sound dramatic, but for me, the sensation was palpable. While many of these companies had extensive programs supporting gender and ethnic diversity, I always felt like I'd better not let my thinking, language, and appearance appear too, shall we say, *unique.* In other words, I'd better stay in line.

As excellent as these corporations were at creating inclusivity programs, they (as well as the government clients I called on) uniformly fostered an absence of the playful, dynamic energy that takes place in my company, which we *intentionally* created via a collaboration of masculine and feminine energies. Perhaps this explains why at these large organizations, I observed relative states of energetic lethargy (instead of enthusiasm) among the otherwise fantastic folks who worked there.

The fact of the matter was that these large corporations were still my bread and butter, so I developed my own process of self-protection to visit their offices. First, I'd pick out a conservative suit—one in which the color, cut, and fabric didn't stand out or distract. Then, after arriving at the meeting, I'd try to remember to say all the *right* abstract corporate jargon and none of the *wrong* things, like curse words, compliments, colloquialisms, and jokes. I would go on pretending to enjoy using incredibly complex lingo to describe simple concepts. Meanwhile, I'd connect with the meeting participants on a very mental or intellectual level, as opposed to belly-laughing or *feeling into* a solution. As soon as it was over, I'd go back to my hotel and take off what felt like my costume.

For the longest time, when I would meet female managers in the defense and consulting industry corporate environments, I often experienced them as slightly standoffish. I finally realized these women were not connecting with me as a typical woman would, and that was precisely the reason why they were given a seat at the table. This is one of the main drivers in my pursuit of advancing *feminine* leadership, because if we don't allow a woman to embody and draw from the energy of her feminine form, how will we ever allow the world to benefit from a female perspective?

Sadly, most corporations (and government agencies) continue to praise inclusivity but reward efforts of conformity and uniformity. Of course, when men tone down their masculine tendencies and women tone down their overtly feminine qualities, it serves the purpose of not attracting unwanted advances or giving off the perception of them. But unfortunately, this dialing back of energy is also hindering one of our primary sources of creative power. I find this entropic tendency causes everyone to meet in the middle, causing achievement, success, and innovation to suffer.

Hopefully, with the success of the #MeToo movement bringing awareness of inappropriate behavior and taking these energies too far, I'm sure the corporate world will figure it out. Fortunately for us entrepreneurs, the same energy that large corporations suppress is what empowers us. In my company, the bulk of my management team is from a certain religion that embodies strict moral compasses due to their beliefs; however, all of us draw upon our natural tendencies for masculine and feminine styles of leadership, which makes the culture more enlivening.

The way I see it, the lack of playful energy and enthusiasm in big corporations is sad. Life is supposed to be full of enjoyment, self-expression, and fulfillment, not monotony, repression, and the denial of one's highest potential. After all, isn't contrast part of what makes life interesting?

For a well-known illustration of what I'm talking about, if you watch the TV show *Shark Tank*, the hosts (investors who became self-made billionaires) achieved their success by *dialing up* their masculine or feminine energy rather than dialing it down. The women on the show seem to play to their uniquely nurturing perspectives rather than trying to entrain to the men's. How do I know this? You can tell just by listening to them and watching the interaction of their mannerisms.

I'm not talking about flirting. They're all alpha males and females who are *not* suppressing their natural magnetic nature in each other's presence. Instead, they seem to channel it into the business at hand. (If you've watched the show and don't recognize this, you may not have spent enough time in large corporate or government agencies to make the comparison.) So it's not surprising that there would be a phenomenon like a glass cliff for women, because merging these energies is part of what *sparks* a passion for success.

We women are team players who enjoy family systems. In my experience, running a company that allows for the promotion of distinctly feminine behaviors is about utilizing masculine and feminine energies to create something more significant. More importantly, in my experiences leading and consulting small to medium-sized companies, I've noticed that our approaches are entirely complementary when balanced.

MASCULINE VERSUS FEMININE HIGH PERFORMANCE

I once had an in-depth conversation with a military general in charge of training the entire United States Army. He shared with me that during the Iraq War, the military began placing females on every village patrol because "they tend to identify enemy insurgents with better accuracy." This type of gender profiling would rarely fly in corporate culture, but when work assignments are the difference between life and death, the leveraging of gender-specific skills is already being utilized by the US military.

If I had to oversimplify my observations about the differences between men and women in the business world (the differences of which are again complementary, in my view), it's that men tend to see things more hierarchically and structurally, and women tend more to see things as an interconnected web. I also tend to notice that men love to make *comparisons*, while women seem to emphasize *distinctions*. A diversity of energies within each person allows each of us to utilize the necessary forms of influence when a situation or circumstance dictates. For instance, *persuasion or consensus-building* may work better than *dominance and absolutism*, and sometimes it's vice versa.

Because feminine leaders don't tend to keep separate the pressures from multiple, simultaneous sources, masculine leaders are seen as more able to compartmentalize. In other words, it's tough for us to be oblivious about certain things as men can seemingly be. The net effect is that if a feminine leader feels like she's in a role that doesn't support her *in all areas of life*, she's less likely to stay with it over the long term.

Conversely, if she can design a leadership role in *her own company* that's organized around the moving parts of her life—and stay inspired—she'll have no problem with a multi-decade assignment of dedication, hard work, and effort. Make no mistake, whether she goes up the ladder in a large corporation or starts her own business, dealing with pressure is imminent. But at least by contrast to working for a big corporation, a leader who starts her own business:

- Never has to worry about promotions and is automatically on the executive team
- Influences the hierarchy of her company immediately and continuously
- Can lead her teams in the manner of her choosing, which may be more inclusive, holistic, and nurturing (if she desires) than anything she has ever seen
- Is more likely to live and work on her terms in an organization she creates from scratch—the perks of which can include flexible hours, etc.
- Can set up leadership communication patterns organized around her style, frequency, and methods of communicating
- Can be fully self-expressed and creative, all while having her feminine energy dialed up, utilized, and leveraged—rather than dialed down to fit into a role
- Has fewer limits to wealth potential than an employee in a system that only promotes and rewards personal sacrifice

My caveat to this list of benefits is that these outcomes aren't guaranteed, and the statistics aren't promising: male entrepreneurs are three and a half times more likely to hit the $1 million revenue mark for startups.[31] This indicates to me that the glass cliff also exists for feminine entrepreneurs, which is one reason why my mission is to help you increase your staying power along the arc of entrepreneurial growth.

In 2012, Forbes.com published an article entitled "A Balance of Both Masculine and Feminine Strengths: The Bottom-Line Benefit." Based on research performed by Catalyst and McKinsey & Company, the report laid out the correlation between gender diversity in leadership and bottom-line results. The Catalyst study demonstrated that companies with more women at senior levels, as well as those that had women serving on boards of directors, posted higher returns. The McKinsey & Company research found that European companies with a higher proportion of women in top management outperformed their competitors on both qualitative and financial measures.[32]

Nearly a decade after first reading the *Forbes* article, I can see why I found it so fascinating—the timing of the article happened to coincide with (and thus reinforce) an idea that had just begun to arise within me that an imbalance of energies was hurting my own company (my employees at the time were all female). By *not* bringing distinctly masculine energy into the top of my organization, my company's bottom line was suffering. A lack of strong accountability for profit levels on projects was just one example. In other words, we weren't sticking our necks out to command higher prices.

Two years later, *Forbes* published another article entitled "Are Feminine Leadership Traits the Future of Business?" The report, which speaks of the gender paradox in innovation, connects the stereotype of male engineers back to the birth of Hewlett-Packard. The irony is that when we think of healthy innovation ecosystems, we think of high levels of connectivity, communication, and collaborative sharing. Well, guess what? These are stereotypically feminine traits. The questions the article ultimately poses are:

If these attributes are so crucial to innovation, why do modern business and political systems not only continue to be dominated by men but place preferential value on stereotypically masculine behaviors? And how does that affect the overall strength of companies and economies?[33]

I can honestly assert that the most critical reason for my global service business surviving several economic downturns (far more effectively than our competitors, I might add) was our team's collaboration, internal communication, and connectivity. The outcome was better problem-solving than if we had deployed a purely logical, siloed approach. In my company's case, the long-term result was that our team always innovated solutions that added value or solved our clients' unmet needs, even if these solutions were outside the boundaries of what we'd seen done before. It was feminine ingenuity at its finest, and that made me very proud.

When masculine and feminine meet, it *creates* something. This is true in biology and business. For example, computers were invented by males, but females invented programming language.[34] There are countless examples of masculine and feminine powers and the sustainable systems they provide when balanced.

When people ask if I'm a feminist, I tell them yes, even though I gave feminism a failing grade, because I do believe in equal opportunities. My focus, however, is more on *women collaborating with men* than competing with the entire group of them on every front, because let's face it— *men will always be better at being men* (and I do love that about them) than women ever will be. And vice versa!

WHAT I'D LIKE TO SEE FEMINISM ACCOMPLISH IN BUSINESS

The issue I've heard hardly anyone talk about concerning corporations, working environments, and hierarchical business systems is that they were all created by men; thus, they naturally put men at an advantage. When women began filling seats in these corporations, and existing workflow and infrastructure elements didn't evolve to incorporate and leverage feminine ways of experiencing, working, and creating, we women started competing with men in the same ways they compete with each other. As a result, we've failed at ascending to top leadership positions and creating balance in both corporate and public power structures.

Why would I possibly say such a thing? *Because the statistics don't lie.*

As of the publication of this book, while the representation of women in senior leadership has increased, women continue to be underrepresented at every level. Although we've taken steps in the right direction, parity remains out of reach—particularly with women of color. According to McKinsey & Company's *Women in the Workplace 2019* report, "About 1 in 5 C-suite executives is a woman—and only 1 in 25 C-suite executives is a woman of color."[35]

To quote Ms. Steinem again, perhaps we should "make the world fit women instead of making women fit the world." I couldn't agree more, and we're going to start with your personal world. I know it's not politically correct to talk about this part of "the diversity issue." Besides being slow to add workflow organization structures around feminine preferences, multinational corporations foster cultures of exhaustion and overwork that even men shouldn't put up with. If it were more acceptable by society for men to feel and demonstrate emotions, they'd tell you how they agonize about choosing a work project over their child's ballet recital or soccer game. But instead, they're willing and expected to be the ones to make the sacrifice.

While she's at work, the average female executive is stressed about what her kids are being exposed to on digital devices while sitting in schools burdened with too many regulations, not enough funding, and active-shooter drills. She might be eating processed food, drinking a tad too much, and not spending time in nature, while making her husband wrong for not seeing all there is to be done around the house.

During the nineteenth and twentieth centuries, when corporate and government leaders were educated and created the hierarchies of our modern capitalist industry, any notion of *feminine leadership mythology* was conspicuously absent. As a result, we leaned on embodying masculine characteristics to be successful in these hierarchies. It's almost as if the phrase "*feminine* leader" was an oxymoron. Hence another major reason that women are not proportionately ascending to positions of success, authority, and influence: female leaders born before the 1990s had virtually *no role models of a feminine leader.*

So here we are all together—swimming in a massively out-of-balance soup. In the process, the average corporate female business leader is likely putting herself in situations in which the chemicals of stress inhibit her ability to perform optimally—which happens to all leaders, both male and female. But female brains are the ones that don't compartmentalize their work from the other parts of their lives as much, and *no one should want us to unless you want to see society go further into the tank.*

BALANCED LEADERSHIP AS A GLOBAL PRIORITY

So far, our currently male-dominated civilization has produced mind-blowing technologies, reduced global hunger, built complex machines to simplify our lives, and sent probes into interstellar space.

The masculine has created energy to power our lives from natural resources, and in turn, has provided relative comfort and convenience to billions across the planet. That's why I believe the domination of masculine accomplishments has not been *at the expense of* what's best for us as women, but rather, these vital things were built partly *in response to* women's needs and desires.

People ask me if I think toxic masculinity exists, and I say, "Of course it does," because power left unchecked creates corruption. There is substantial suppression, violence, and displacement around the world resulting from the separation-based aspect of masculine leadership, even if the very infrastructure upon which global commerce operates was designed and built primarily by it.

I can't understand how countries can hold each other accountable concerning nuclear weapons, trade deficits, and treaties, yet at the same time can be oblivious to fundamental human rights for women. Why do we sanction or wage war on some countries for committing human rights atrocities, while in other cases, we blatantly ignore that females are killed, mutilated, sterilized, raped, abandoned as infants, or treated like property? And these are the same nations where we provide aid or conduct business.

To solve these atrocities and other large-scale societal ailments, humanity must remember and leverage women's unique contribution while recruiting the absolute best and brightest ones into the top levels of global leadership—*pronto*. For the success and prosperity of humanity, we need to act swiftly to put an end to *both* misogyny (hatred of women) and misandry (hatred of men). We can do this by bringing our hearts and minds together to resolve conflict, poverty, and the same divisive problems that have plagued us for centuries in new and novel ways.

Whether it's corporate social responsibility programs, awakened policy changes toward human rights, or blocks against selling goods in countries that allow the oppression of their female population or that have harmful environmental practices, the reach of multinational businesses can uniquely effect change across multiple cultures, economies, and political environments at once.

At a more fundamental level than is currently acknowledged, business leaders shape conversations (or lack thereof) around these topics, which gives us the power to solve many of the earth's current problems—too many of which were created by unbridled profit motives in the first place.

I'm not blaming masculinity for the world's issues, and I don't see complaining about men and the patriarchy as being valid. That kind of oppositional thinking doesn't solve problems. Instead, it only leads to more separation. We need CEOs and executives who approach problems from a new level of thinking. An *inspired* way of thinking.

CHAPTER 2

CEO-SHIP AS AN INSPIRED FEMININE LEADER

Because you picked up this book, chances are you're a current or future entrepreneur, which makes you a current or future CEO. Therefore, I'm going to be talking to you like one. Whether you're an employee dreaming about being a business owner, a solopreneur who wants to scale up, or a high-performance founder who's already playing her game, I want to help you embrace more of the natural CEO abilities you possess but aren't utilizing, and help you step into new skills with as much ease and grace as you would an Armani suit.

The difference between my coaching and what you learn through being promoted up the ranks in someone else's company is that *you can design your business to serve you* so you can stay inspired to be in service to it. Being an Inspired Feminine Leader (IFL) is imperative for getting through the inevitable high-pressure circumstances that will occur over multiple decades of your leadership career.

When a woman's life is in alignment with her truest needs, everyone wins—from her clients to her employees to her family. It's one of the most valuable but underrated accomplishments of an IFL's journey. When you move your state of being from a sense of longing for relief all the time to one of being fulfilled, you'll experience a deep, relaxing trust of your instincts while staying in the high-performance mode that enables you to add zeros to your bottom line.

As promised, I want to show you how living your best possible life is not only a destination but *the path* to success, especially in the mercilessly competitive world of business. However, I have some good news and bad news for you. First, the bad news.

When you begin breaking the mold of your old self, some people—perhaps even those who you're close with—are going to feel uncomfortable with who you're becoming, and they won't be able to meet you where you are energetically. As a result, they may fall out of your orbit, while others may try to take you out or pull you down to accommodate their comfort zone. Therefore, my advice is to read the following chapters without regard for what people might think if you implement these practices—at least at first.

The good news is that the more you fine-tune your game through the expansion of your focus and conscious awareness, the more you're going to learn to spot these energy vampires. When you do recognize them, you'll be able to see that they're simply interference patterns in your field. No, I'm not talking about physics or football (even though I'm from Texas, so we're gonna be talkin' some football soon). I'm talking about people who interfere with your vision.

If you haven't already noticed, I like to call entrepreneurship by a nickname: *the game*. The game is about achieving purposeful, playful, and joyful productivity while you're *moving money, moving products, or moving people—all of which, in a sense, is the movement of energy.* In this way, I want to light the path of your journey with analogies, stories, and hard-won wisdom.

What I also think you might find useful is the insight I gained as to what *not* to do during my trials and tribulations serving as a supplier to the world's largest corporations and as a government contractor. As a turnaround consultant helping underperforming companies install new leadership and management systems, I was also witness to some very unhealthy leadership behaviors, which made everyone in the companies miserable and adversely affected profits.

In the next chapters, I'll help reactivate your curiosity, internal alignment, and creative abilities in an actionable, professional way. You'll also get answers to the top questions asked by participants of my entrepreneurship seminars. Finally, I'll reveal shortcuts to help you circumvent gaps in your skills and crush it like a classically trained CEO— because serving others and bringing balance to the planet isn't enough to sustain anyone in the battle of business ownership. We, as leaders, also enjoy some combination of money, respect, recognition, and/or winning.

The benefits of being an IFL go well beyond the material and egoic realm, and include accessing heightened states of awareness from which we must operate to passionately serve our clients and employees in our unique way. Over time, we get to experience playing the game as a reliable method for "waking up" in a lucid dream that few people (outside of performers, athletes, etc.) have the opportunity to access.

BE INSPIRED

The Latin root of *inspiration* comes from *inspirare*, which means to "blow into, excite, inflame." Research in 2003 showed that inspiration has a major effect on a person's outcomes in life.[36] Psychologists Todd M. Thrash and Andrew J. Elliot found that inspired people report being more intrinsically motivated and have greater belief in their own abilities, higher self-esteem, and optimism—all of which enhances work performance.

In my experience, when it comes to accomplishing anything of substance, inspiration trumps motivation any day. Inspiration has been shown to facilitate progress toward goals,[37] and this relationship is reciprocal, so goal progress subsequently predicts future goal inspiration.[38]

For me, inspiration is akin to inhaling the divine spark of creation, and it's been this way for as long as I can remember. As a child who could never seem to stop daydreaming, I've always sought connection with that experience where the veil of other dimensions intersects with the reality we experience through our senses.

It's been said that inspiration is associated with the sixth "chakra" (one of seven energy centers of the body), which is the area located between the eyebrows. Scientists are now calling chakras energy centers, because within each area exists about forty thousand plexuses of neurons, making each chakra—or energy center—a virtual mini brain.[39] At the center of the sixth energy center is the *pineal gland*. This endocrine gland lies in between the two halves of the brain, and it has extensive nerve connections to both.[40]

The pineal gland has a colorful story that can be traced all the way back to the ancient Egyptians,[41] and yet among our endocrine glands, its function was discovered last. Dubbed the "third eye," the origin of its nickname comes from its connection to light (it's responsible for our circadian rhythm[42]) and its ability to pick up information beyond the visible light spectrum.[43]

Because we receive information from this sixth energy center that we cannot pick up with our other senses, we could think of it as our antenna to the divine, or at least the *unseen*. This antenna awakens us to what's possible in the infinite field of potential, and it allows us to create (and lead) from a higher level of mind.

Here's the only problem. Much of humanity is operating from our lower mind, which is designed to ensure survival in a hostile setting. The lower mind's decisions and viewpoints then start a cycle of egoic domination in which fear and separation are the preeminent drivers. This lower mind craves sameness and status quo, and thus will prevail as our operating system unless we transcend it by raising our consciousness. While raising consciousness is outside the scope of this book, you may have gathered by now that I've written it to support you in achieving higher, expanded states of consciousness through the vehicle of business ownership. This is one way we can transcend lower-mind dominance.

Inspiration gives us a place to focus beyond our survival-based instincts when the going gets rough, as we women are arguably socialized (and built) to retreat when in harm's way—*unless we're fighting for something bigger than ourselves.* For each of us, that divine spark—what we want *to be filled with and used for*—is going to be different, and no one can tell you what that is but yourself.

What I can tell you with confidence is that if a leader doesn't create the life conditions and practices that allow her to access states of inspiration, she'll either have to work harder due to diminished creative powers, or her leadership career is going to be short-lived.

I feel incredibly blessed to have made a measurably positive impact on a number of families and on some rather significant projects by organizing my life around being an IFL. You can probably trace back your own success to the decisions you've made while in a state of inspiration. Because when you're in that state, you're more inclined to make choices that create the life you love.

DESIGN A LIFE YOU LOVE

An IFL designs her business game around the whole of her desires, which serves as a blueprint for her longevity in the leadership game. That's why I'd like to recommend again organizing your business to serve *you*—not just the other way around. If not, you can expect burnout and general dissatisfaction.

One of my mentors used to say, "If you aren't getting what you want, you're subconsciously preventing others from getting what they want." Besides doing everyone around you a favor, getting clear on what you desire serves another purpose—you can consider it your prize for playing and winning your game. When you encounter challenges and seemingly harmless temptations that make quitting seem easier than getting desperately creative, keeping your eye on that prize provides your inspiration.

What's more, if you give yourself permission (and accept that you deserve) the reward, you can then resonate with having it, thereby increasing your chances of success. Einstein has been attributed as saying, "Everything is energy, and that's all there is to it. Match the frequency of the reality you want, and you cannot help but get that reality. It can be no other way."

Being in alignment with your desired outcomes is so vital in my opinion; it's actually how I measure being high performance. If *you* are operating at high performance, and you believe that loving your life is available to you as a constant state, you'll attract other people who hang out on that same vibe.

THE MYTH OF WORK-LIFE BALANCE

Until recently, the conversation regarding lifting females to higher levels in corporate business leadership centered around the individual's work-life balance rather than balancing masculine/feminine energies within companies. So what, exactly, is the corporate world's notion of work-life balance? Throughout my career, in hearing corporate leaders speak about it, work-life balance is like an algebraic equation whereby kids, relationships, career, health, social life, and domestic duties are each given the appropriate amount of attention and energy.

This conceptual framework for balance has been doomed from the start because, as women, we energetically *merge all of our priorities*. We feel we must have at least a bit of our attention on each critical item at once. "Out of sight, out of mind" generally doesn't work very well.

As I mentioned earlier, ninety days after I started my business, I realized I was having twins. One year later, I had five employees and three babies (nursing two of them, with all three of them in diapers) at my house. I had no choice but to learn how to be a mom *and* an entrepreneur in tandem. I'd even go so far as to say that the business game deserves partial credit for my kids turning out as well as they did—not only because of the flexible schedule and support system it afforded me, but it also kept me in constant creation mode.

So while my business allowed me flexibility and support, it did *not* allow me time to wallow in moods, victimhood, complaints, gossip, or other unproductive games I witnessed my social peers playing. The challenges I created for myself required superhuman resolve, passion, and endurance. This is why it's essential to focus on being supported in the areas that are impactful to *you*, such as nutrition, spiritual practice, movement, caring for kids, and help around the house.

Rather than working on balance, if you end up feeling used up, drained, or like you've somehow gotten off track, I invite you to briefly consider these questions or take out a piece of paper and really dig into them:

- What do I really need? Is it something more t' been willing to admit?
- Am I in touch with my deepest desires, or am I ignoring them? What are they?
- Am I following my highest choice in nutrition? Sleep? Self-care?
- Am I moving in a way that my body really enjoys at least a few times a week?
- Besides the love of the game and being in service, what's the big payoff to being an entrepreneur? Am I giving myself that payoff? Or pushing it too far into the future? What's missing in my business supporting my aliveness?

If any of these somehow make you feel helpless or hopeless, explore them more deeply in a notebook or a journal. The process of writing very often has a way of shaking things loose that you otherwise couldn't see.

I've observed that feminine entrepreneurs are more likely to feel they have to choose between maintaining each and every one of their individual relationships or attending to their business projects. Over time, if their personal lives are not thriving, statistics show they're more likely to revert back, turning away from persistent business challenges to support the ecosystems of their personal lives. As you'll come to embrace by the end of this book, to want to opt out is not a weakness but, rather, a result of "seeing all that we see" (or empathically sensing) and still being able to function.

I can't tell you it's wrong to drop off the glass cliff of entrepreneurship when you honestly think it's the best course of action, but I can show you how to avoid it. Because girls are still programmed by society to be more *proactively* self-conscious than boys, they might be more likely to overanalyze their entrepreneurial choices. I've certainly seen this in myself.

All of this is to emphasize that once you launch your firm, there should be no going back, at least until you decide to sell it, the preparation for which is another topic for another book. Therefore, part of being an IFL is to regularly call upon people as resources for ongoing support and encouragement, people who are equally talented or better, many of whom will be men who can help you compartmentalize your way out of feeling overwhelmed. Just know you don't have to go about it alone even though it is a lonely path.

THE PARADOX OF INTENSITY

Whether conducting feminine entrepreneurship seminars or leading female team members for twenty-five years, I find that women in business love intensity as much as anyone. That's why I'd like to distinguish intensity from pressure and have my readers understand why it matters.

While pressure is a motivating force for some because it means that expectations are high, it can also carry unintended consequences with an IFL if it's the type of pressure that doesn't relent over time. Why? Because no matter how genius, experienced, or badass she is, being under pressure causes her to hyperfocus, and if she is not supported adequately at home or at work, parts of her life start to suffer. Of course, this happens to men, but when it happens to a feminine leader's life, she eventually reacts differently because she does not separate the various priorities.

So, while most of us leaders get a little high from pressure every now and then, for IFLs, it should be consumed in moderation. We prefer our intensity to come from *playing*, not fighting. Fighting, even energetically and not kinetically, takes us out of the game because our bodies aren't built for fighting. That's why, when pushed, it's in our nature to fight more unfairly (usually with words, directly or behind someone's back), and this can *destroy* the game over time.

When it comes to *playing* in a competitive game, however, I would choose a team of female players any day of the week. If you have never seen a competitive, collaborative, and very feminine team play to win, please go see a high school volleyball championship game at your next opportunity. These girls haven't been demoralized by masculine, hard-driving coaches. They're still "all girl," and yet they're fierce about winning. That ferocity arises mostly out of the desire to not let their teammates (aka friends) down. They're hugging, shouting commands, falling down hard, and getting back up swiftly. And like all good competitors, *they know they're playing against themselves.*

One thing I wish more people would recognize is how feminine leaders bring more play and innocence to the business game, no matter how intense things get. I guess the reason we're that way is that in order to be a mother of a toddler or infant, we have to be extremely patient and understanding. Even on the days we don't feel like it, we're called to display compassion for dealing with humans who have no clue.

BE INSPIRING

Within her own home, a mother in her natural state is an innate expert at teaching children how to speak, how to tie shoes, how to eat with a spoon, and how to clean up after themselves. How do moms do it? They create little games with rewards and celebrations, which is exactly how to inspire people in a small to medium-sized company. In my company, the masculine managers have picked up on the value of these games ("side games," they call them). By creating them, they maintain elevated energy on our teams, as they show up day after day to the playground of business.

In my experience, it's the feminine managers who are more likely to inspire others when their team members accomplish difficult tasks behind the scenes. They are quick to acknowledge unsung heroes for victories and to make sure the person who accomplishes the "thankless" tasks gets recognized. If you don't have feminine managers in your company, you're missing out on one of the greatest resources of inspiration a company can draw from.

That said, I am still a huge fan of balancing the energies, so you do need the counterbalance of the masculine, which can be implemented by either gender. Our leaders with masculine energies will tend to make sure we're not just having a lovefest (yes, our culture is that good) and that we are maintaining our focus on driving the numbers versus just "playing office." They're less concerned about whether everybody feels warm and fuzzy. Both styles are important and contribute to an inspired workforce, *just like both styles are important in raising inspired children at home, even if these energies have to be exhibited by a single parent.*

LEAD WITH LOVE

In modern terms, effectively balanced leadership is about hearts *and* minds. I've heard some describe balanced leadership as being "heart-centered." An online search of business and government leaders being known as heart-centered, balanced, or kind yields almost no results. The divisive, vitriolic atmosphere of our current media-driven culture makes heart-centered leaders want to remain in the background. You would think they don't exist, but it's more likely they just aren't being recognized as such.

Unfortunately, the heart-centered leader goes unrecognized as an actual leader and is more often simply known as a "public figure." Think Maya Angelou, Brené Brown, Arianna Huffington, and so on. But being heart-centered coincides with the newest trends in influencing people. When it comes to business, a heart-centered leader respects all people, not just profits, while still meeting the stringent standards required in the game of business. When a heart-centered leader interacts with others, she (or he) *leads with love.*

Leading with love isn't a passive, acquiescent activity. It takes passion and a fire in your belly to get people to suspend habitual ways of thinking and align with your big-picture vision. In addition to leading, you also have to reliably and systematically deal with your own demons of doubt and/or dysfunction.

In other words, to lead with love, you have to be a badass motherf*cker.

The reason I have taken part in executive education, personal development, and transformational training, and why I've been a coach and facilitator for more than twenty-five years is that leading from our hearts *and* being high-performance requires that we use special methods, which I will share in later chapters.

As human beings growing up and growing older, via pain, trauma, loss, and so on, developing fragmented parts of ourselves is unavoidable. If we are aware of these wounds, our business is constantly presenting us with opportunities to heal by bringing new thinking to the repeating patterns we seem to attract again and again.

Interestingly enough, the work environment is one of those places where repeating patterns and healing opportunities emerge—not only for you as the owner but for all of your employees. Operating a business is going to put you in a coaching role to help people metabolize your team members' lower-mind instincts for protecting, defending, fighting, or fleeing. In other words, you'll be putting your employees in work situations where they may end up in a state of fight or flight, and then you'll have to coach them out of it.

These situations provide opportunities for you to walk them up the ladder of conscious awareness so they can confront these *perceived* threats with rational responses. Once again, the key to this is to lead with love.

Use the word "love" with them, tell them you love them all (in a group setting), and well...just *be love*. Love the diversity and uniqueness offered by your employees, clients, and suppliers. When a team member does something great, tell that person, "I *love* what you're doing and what you're providing to this company (or project)."

Whether you have let someone go for the good of the organization or you're promoting someone and enhancing their life, leading with love is a job that requires *fierce commitment*. It doesn't guarantee that you'll be loved in return. It's a form of integrity in which you take on a complex web of simultaneous needs that are in the best interest of your employees, yourself, your clients, and even your suppliers. It is an immense, paradoxical, sometimes mindf*ck of an undertaking.

Some leaders I know, especially masculine ones, cannot even wrap their minds around the concept of loving leadership and instead prefer to keep love separate from work, which is a double-edged sword (as we'll discuss later). But Inspired Feminine Leaders, along with the men who are promoted within my company, can focus on both. Leading with love sometimes feels illogical, but it's what makes our business games a path of personal evolution, and it's a source code (like the code that makes up a computer's operating system) for bringing out the best in ourselves and our teams.

THE SPIRITUAL PATH OF ENTREPRENEURSHIP

In addition to heart-centered leadership being a path for healing, it also has the tendency to turn one's business into a spiritual path by revealing some of the unseen forces at play in our lives. One of those forces is the difference between *doing* and *being*.

On TV and the internet—hundreds of times per day—advertisers pay millions of dollars to try to turn us (especially women) into bigger and bigger consumers, programming us into believing that when we *have* a certain thing, we can *be* a certain thing—and that will make us feel whole and complete. This is complete nonsense. The *being* comes first.

What causes your *being* is a *choice* of "what shall be" in your life—powerfully spoken, intentionally thought of, and consistently supported by your actions, conversations, and the focus of your attention. Therefore, if you choose to passionately vent something like, "Ugh, we always get paid late by that vendor," guess what will happen? Conversely, if you choose to enthusiastically assert, "My employees always have my back and my customers' best interest at heart," you're empowering and trusting them to live into that belief (along with expecting them to perform).

Every moment, in our thoughts, decisions, and actions as a leader, we're faced with the question "Who do we want to be?" The sum of these choices heavily influences where your company will succeed and where it will fail. The reason comes down to a simple idea: where you place your attention dictates where your team's attention will go. And where your team's attention goes, so goes their energy. Saying that thoughts become things is a bit cliché, but I've found over many years that the quality of my thoughts leads to my outcomes, both directly and indirectly.

If you've never seen the movie *The Legend of Bagger Vance*, the story about a golfer who has fallen into a severe slump when a caddy (with guru-like coaching capabilities) appears to help him, skip to the next paragraph—I don't want to ruin it for you. I love this movie, and the reason I mention it is that I relate to the golfer (played by Matt Damon), who, to get out of his slump, is forced to learn to consciously connect to the idea of a quantum field of potentials versus focusing on the distance or accuracy of each swing. He had to *put his attention on the potential in which the ball goes in*, then align with that outcome. Fortunately for you, your business is going to show you on a moment-by-moment basis a reflection of whether you're aligned with achieving your highest possible potential.

Modern science has merged with traditional spiritual philosophies to suggest that at all times, whether we realize it or not, we're interdimensional beings creating in the quantum field. When you work with your connection to this quantum field to create wholeness out of a disparate set of demands, you will create a business machine that counteracts entropy (which is the gradual decline into disorder). As you do so, you'll also be counteracting entropy within yourself while discovering new levels of mental, physical, and spiritual coherence.

MIND OVER MATTER

To be an IFL means to operate outside the habits (formerly seen as laws) of physics in a way that others may not understand. It is our five senses of sight, hearing, touch, smell, and taste that deceive us into the idea or notion of ourselves as separate from *all that is*. Because the modern human puts so much stock in these senses, we've been tricked into believing we can accurately measure what constitutes reality by using them. Whereas, without our senses, there would only be awareness. (Imagine if you couldn't see, hear, taste, touch, or smell. You would still be "an awareness.")

At the quantum level, however, the physicality of reality changes. It is said that the atom is made up of 99.999999 percent empty space. Everything is made up of atoms, and that space in the atom is not emptiness but energy. Science is increasingly pointing to a notion that this energy is "waiting" to be directed by an observer or consciousness—which is each and every one of us. This is the field of energy that presides over and unifies all other governing laws of the physical world. Thus, at the quantum level, we are presumably influencing matter with our minds.

Since, as Einstein said, "The field is the sole governing body of the particle," we can accept that as IFLs, we are called to take responsibility for creating the quality of our energetic fields and then dealing with what those fields produce. In my experience, this translates into utilizing three profoundly important leadership tactics:

1. Treating people as though "there is only one of us." The Golden Rule was based on a scripture out of Matthew 7:12, which said, "So in everything, do to others what you would have them do to you, for this sums up the Law and the Prophets." I'm not exactly a gospel preacher, since I've never read the entire Bible, and I embrace tenets from a multitude of religions; however, I believe that this message can be construed not only as "do unto others" but as "whatever you're doing to others, you are doing to yourself." When I am feeling separation from someone with whom I am committed to feeling unity, prior to speaking my truth, I sometimes say a silent decree: "God in me speaks to God in you."
2. Speaking consciously (as we cover more extensively in chapter 5) dictates that you understand that your lan-

guage creates energy and sends a signal to the infinite field of potentials.

3. Innovatively using your imagination (which we cover at length in chapter 6)—essentially giving yourself permission to receive what you have carefully selected as your desires—instead of manifesting drama, negativity, and unworkability by being sloppy with your repetitive thoughts. By accessing higher states of consciousness through your imagination, you're *placing your desired outcomes into your timeline*, so to speak, rather than working so hard that you subconsciously push them further out.

For decades, business books and spiritual texts have asked leaders to memorize sets of rules or dogmas as to how we should think or act to be successful. In doing so, in some aspects, we became subservient to the logical part of the brain and made the imagination secondary, which is a tragedy because it's our feelings and imagination that connect our awareness to that infinite field.

And so, leaders became disconnected from the world of feelings. Instead, they became protective of a set of paradigms concerning what high performance is supposed to look like. Instead of leading, they look for inconsistencies with regard to how processes and people should behave in relation to certain rules.

This type of thinking causes the mind of the average leader to become a right/wrong judgment machine, which kills inspiration, happiness, vitality, connection, and love. To do everything the "right way" is a huge waste of life force. When you approach problems purely from a linear perspective instead of opening yourself up to the synchronicity, ease, and grace, it takes ten or twenty times longer to reach goals.

That said, I find it's easier for IFLs to consider these theories of leadership and experiment with them than it is for other leaders. So it's not something you have to convince others into believing. For example, as a human who is in a feminine embodiment, I recognize that I possess a deeper sensitivity, a kind of radar or intuition, that many of my masculine colleagues do not. By recognizing and utilizing that sensitivity, I bring to my male counterparts a different perspective—one that more often comes without separation, charge, and judgment.

ATTRACT SYNCHRONICITIES

Creating your world as a matter of intentional choice, shifting into a new set of circumstances with intentional language and vision, and spontaneously fulfilling your desires is *not* woo-woo voodoo. It is about realizing (real-eyes-ing) potentials by bringing your awareness to "what's possible" without being able to see it—rather than being limited by your construct of "what is."

One way to realize potentiality is to be *allowing*—to give yourself permission to receive that which you seek. This is how we get aligned with ourselves in addition to how we gain alignment within our teams. Your teams are only going to reach for the goals they give themselves permission to achieve. If I cannot feel gratitude for something in advance, I know I'm somehow resisting it, and I may not even recognize it when the opportunity shows itself. As an example, my sales team will not notice sales opportunities they can't imagine achieving.

As a coach, I've seen untold numbers of clients make a clear vision and then subconsciously push away or ignore the very opportunity when it showed up. Why? Because they were blind to a solution, situation, or event that didn't fit into their paradigm of possibility. On the other hand, if you stay connected to your vision, you'll start noticing what Joseph Jaworski referred to in his book *Synchronicity: The Inner Path to Leadership* as "predictable miracles."[44]

When you open yourself up to this way of being, you'll start feeling more connected to that invisible field of potentials, and you'll likely begin experiencing uncanny coincidences. Situations will arrange themselves around your new vision, the people you need to show up in your network will appear out of nowhere, and opportunities will seem to come out of thin air.

It took me more than fifteen years to embody the concept that by "not doing," I can create (or make things happen) much more easily than if I use effort, force, strain, and struggle. Besides working less hard, there are some other great benefits to playing in the quantum realm. Here are the four main ones:

1. *Your life flows and your results come to you with more ease.* You experience synchronicities of greater magnitude. You're living as a vision of the future instead of a victim of the past, and because your emphasis is on consciously choosing thoughts and actions that are in alignment with your vision, you break patterns of living

in survival. Instead, you relax into thriving—even when the game gets intense.

2. *You start to forgive situations, actions, and people in advance.* You get a more functional context for life and its ups and downs. You transcend worrying about other people's reactions and their egoic concerns; you do a lot less explaining and stop worrying about fixing everything.

3. *You stop complaining.* Whereas before you leaked energy through complaining (and received attention for it), now you conserve energy by taking responsibility. Before, you wouldn't think twice about mixing up a stress cocktail (adrenaline or cortisol, anyone?) and then ride that buzz of intensity. Now you feel drained after a rant. You can sense that your thoughts have energy, so more often, you practice not putting those negative impulses into existence and instead start to feel gratitude more often.

4. *You have more moments of joy sparked by a deep, ecstatic appreciation for being alive.* You've started to see everyone and everything as *ahhhlllright*. These moments might be intentionally triggered through activities leading to a sense of oneness, such as meditation and movement, or by having coaches who show you the way. What's even better, the increased frequency of these elevated emotions will bring you into brain coherence, which aligns your intention and heart intelligence. (If you want to learn more about this, check out HeartMath. org). If joyful feelings occur more frequently, especially when you least expect, then focusing your intent on mastering elevated emotions is working.

Since we've covered some of the things that make being an Inspired Feminine Leader different from the average leader, let's now dive into how she actually plays the business game!

CHAPTER 3

GET YOUR HEAD IN THE GAME

"Go to the mound," my coach said, pointing to me.

For the chubby eleven-year-old version of me, my fast-pitch softball career began as a benchwarmer who sometimes played outfielder. Since the team's only pitcher had decided not to show up, we were short on pitchers for batting practice.

The first thing my coach showed me was how to grab the ball by the laces and how to situate my feet on the rubber rectangle covered in dust. I looked down at my fingers, which could barely hold on to the ball, then lobbed it in the general direction of the batter. I continued to fumble through batting practice in a discombobulated, uncertain state. *I've never even been in the infield, much less on the pitcher's mound*, I remember thinking.

It was a whole different vibe. *This is where the action is*, I thought to myself.

To my young mind, I figured it would be a brief rotation, first because I was terrible, and second because we had another (far better) pitcher. Much to my surprise, however, the next day, I was once again placed on the pitcher's mound.

It was not long afterward that our starting pitcher loaded the bases during an actual game, which resulted in me being placed in the pitcher's circle. Parents were cheering, the other team was chanting against me, my coaches crossed their arms, and Mom and Dad looked on nervously. The next several batters, all of them athletic, were actually my schoolmates. I was fresh meat, and they were swinging for the fences.

It was there on the pitcher's mound where I learned that *on a moment-to-moment basis, my outcomes are completely influenced by my thoughts*...and over the next seven years as an all-star athlete, I continued to experience this in a relentlessly visceral manner.

On a macro level, what I learned from playing sports was how to:

1. *Change my thinking instantaneously to change my results, especially when escaping the situation feels safer.* (Special thanks to the coaches who refused to pull me out of a game after walking four batters in a row, even though I wanted out.) Once you pass the point of no return in starting a business, you'll be in this state of being for a large portion of your life.
2. *Determine if your team is going to win or lose simply based on the way they walk onto the field before the game even starts and shift the mood as required.* Because our limbic systems are open systems, meaning we entrain to each

other's moods—our mental makeup can be the difference between team cohesiveness and team sabotage. On our team, my catcher and I were the ones that got everyone out of their heads—whether we had to scream, motivate, cry, or otherwise enroll teammates into the idea that demoralizing our opponents would be more fun than slumping into a loss.

3. *Get a team remotivated after being humiliated by their own massive errors and stupidly small mistakes.* Performing a soul retrieval on a team isn't just for shamans (which we cover in chapter 5).

4. *Psychologically dominate when needed.* Be authentic as an IFL, but *always* make it self-evident that you have a spine. Posturing is about being kind and open-hearted while at the same time being proactive in letting people know you are not to be messed with. This is only to be used when extremely necessary, for it will swing you into your masculine side for weeks, not to mention open you up to negative blowback.

5. *Rally the team behind you because you don't have the clarity to "paint the corners that day."* I have found this to be one of the most consistent shortcomings of all leaders. When you're feeling dull, you will benefit from enrolling your team to step up and support you even more. (Painting the corners is a term used to describe when a pitcher finesses the ball into the corners of a strike zone, making the batter swing and miss.)

6. *Practice the fundamentals enough times so that when the time comes, you are ready to execute on them.* With the bases loaded and a full count on the batter, there's nothing quite like winning a championship with a perfectly executed defensive triple play. The only way to do that is to master the basics.

If you've ever trained for sports or some type of performance art, you know the difference between ordinary thinking and game-time (or show-time) thinking. If you haven't designed your interview process to uncover this ability in prospective team members, I strongly recommend doing so with the goal of comprising at least 25 percent of your team with people who have this background.

When the proverbial sh*t hits the fan, as it will from time to time, if you can't rise to the occasion to create that on-demand, laser-like, game-winning focus—the same focus that separates the amateurs from the pros—you're going to get benched, or worse, the game will kick you out. In business, that translates to *going out of business* or *voluntarily quitting*. The good news is, as your coach, I'm here to tell you how to stay in the game. The first rule is to give up being in control and surrender into uncertainty.

SURRENDER INTO UNCERTAINTY

Whether you're a player or a spectator, the most exciting aspect of a super-competitive game is the element of surprise, right? Well, high performance is full of surprises, and if we learn to love this aspect of it, we can better respond. In fact, I believe that loving uncertainty and learning how to harness the feelings it produces into actionable implementation is a hallmark of successful entrepreneurship. When you can love whatever is happening (versus resisting or hating it), you are operating at a whole new level. From there, you can dictate the course of the game rather than merely reacting or "putting out fires," which in ordinary jobs is what most of us get trained to do.

Anytime you feel a tinge of anxiousness arising within you, use a slow, intentional breath to let your body know you're safe, so you can continue making decisions from a higher level of mind. Know that your fear is likely a protective mechanism containing a combination of old thoughts, habits, programs, and beliefs, as well as the correlating internal chemistry they create in your body.

As a CEO leading a company that is facing uncertainty, if you don't know where your organization is going next, I recommend saying, "This is where we are *right now.*" Your team will feel more confident that you are at least acknowledging the current reality. In saying, "This is where we are," you put your players at ease with what they are perceiving. If you don't provide verbal clarifications frequently, *especially* in times of uncertainty, your team will make up their own stories while thinking you're either unaware or holding back.

However, as I've emphasized, I recommend saying, "I don't know," when you don't know. Many "old-school" leaders are still of the mindset that a leader has to appear all-knowing. I am entertained by colleagues who readily tell me, "This is the way it is," about something when we both know we're all making it up as we go along. It's good to have instincts, and it's fun to make decrees about the way things are, but if you want to win consistently, *stay curious.* The larger the game, the more valuable a *willingness to be wrong* is.

When playing a big game, I've found that sometimes it's hard to tell the difference between fear or anxiety and exhilaration. These defining moments are catalysts that throw us into either *asset thinking* or *liability thinking*, which I learned as a participant in an executive roundtable program via a company called Gap International. You can think of these terms as describing the qualities of your internal winner dialogue versus the internal loser dialogue. Liability thinking consists of internal dialogues as default or automatic programs you pick up along the way, but there are ways to override the loser ones.

Asset thinking is what the best football coaches know how to bring out in their locker-room pep talks, so by the time the team walks back on the field, they've transformed their focus from negative self-talk to "Let's go kick some ever-lovin' ass." Coaches do this by alchemizing the same charged energy (usually from being pissed off) that the players walked into the locker room with and converting it to a positive force by using the power of *choice*. Some examples of the power of choice in asset thinking are:

- "We *can* do this."
- "We *are* the ones for this job."
- "We *will* rise to this occasion."
- "This *will* be our finest hour."

These statements look rather simple in writing, but if you use your imagination on the feeling behind each one, you start to understand the power of this basic method. In my experience, the most compelling way to change your thinking (your inner dialogue) is through a practice I've mentioned called "conscious language" (your outer dialogue), which I will cover in chapter 5. Until then, let's look at more ways of keeping your head in the game.

COMFORT ZONE VERSUS GENIUS ZONE

For IFLs to walk that fine line between fear and faith while staying resilient in the face of the unknown and even embracing it, it's important to recognize the distinction between one's comfort zone and her genius zone. The absolute finest outcomes ever created by me or my executive team have been done from our genius zone.

When you're in your comfort zone, you're coasting; when you're in your genius zone, you're in your true function. In my experience, a company's long-term success depends on organizing roles and processes to push everyone out of their comfort zones and into their genius zones, including yourself, as the business owner.

Your comfort zone likes the status quo, although it's different for everyone. Oddly, I know CEOs whose comfort zone is absolute chaos. For others, it's following a strict plan. In both cases, the CEO's comfort zone will be a default weakness of the organization. How can I say such a thing? Because comfort is the enemy of achieving greatness, mastering resilience, and doing anything extraordinary.

Everyone has a comfort zone, including the highest-performing entrepreneurs. When you find yourself in yours for too long and you can't seem to generate a burning platform (some sort of situation that creates a sense of urgency), it can be a good idea to *put more at stake*. Why not purchase that car you've always wanted? Or hire an executive assistant and two new salespeople? Or go on an outrageously expensive vacation? Or commit yourself to buy three rental properties in eighteen months? Now you're going to have to get creative to figure out how to pay for it. This strategy isn't for everyone, but sometimes it's necessary for veteran leaders to ante up to get ourselves unstuck.

As for being in your genius zone, first, you have to get feedback from a curious, reliable observer to see what *really lights you up*, then you need to put awareness on what types of activities and accomplishments *make you feel stronger*, in addition to knowing *what you're good at*. There are things I'm good at that I also hate doing, so I don't include that in my genius zone. Why? Because if you hate something, you're going to subconsciously mess it up.

My genius zone is found in corporate-level selling. When I was prepping for meetings where my biggest financial deals were at stake, I had to completely transcend my ego, self-consciousness, worries, ordinary routine, and so on. This might have me spending twenty hours to prepare for a twenty-minute presentation. Every word had to hit a particular note within the right octave. None of it could seem contrived, but rather, it had to be real, accurate, and straight to the point.

Even if I were in dire financial straits, to align my current self with my imagined future self as a successful contract awardee, I would buy an impeccably tailored suit and an insanely expensive pair of shoes. It was my way of tuning my entire being into the desired outcome and embodying my future self, who already had the new client. It wasn't about being fake in any way or simply dressing for the role you want—as the saying goes. It was about bending time and space by becoming their service partner *in advance of signing* the contract.

These big opportunities required me to operate from a

higher state of consciousness. It was then my responsibility to share in these kinds of intense training grounds by delegating future opportunities to my team so they could gain experience doing the same. When you empower your teams to handle high-stakes situations in which they benefit from being the hero or learning from the failures, you have a chance of getting to the wealthy visionary role.

INTUITION, INSTINCTS, AND TIMING

One of the most powerfully underutilized tools of feminine entrepreneurs is intuition. IFLs not only deploy their intuition; they listen to the intuition of team members whose gut feelings about these things can be trusted. Between intuition, instincts, and timing, those in touch with their feminine energy have the advantage.

I had a mentor who once said, "When you can see the head of the snake, you know the tail is always going to follow." As humans, we often like to pretend we didn't see the head of the snake, don't we? Maybe we're ruminating on something that feels "off," and yet we take no action in the face of our resistance. So the paradox is to base your actions on facts while trusting your feelings as well.

In your company, if you have an intuitive sense about something that isn't exactly observable, it's a good practice to make a soft verbal inquiry, as long as you do so without making everyone paranoid. I think it's healthy to have an executive team member that does a deep dive into subjects on your behalf without questioning why you are asking. This person needs to be *highly objective by nature*. Anything less will stir up drama and intrigue, which you don't need.

Our culture still rewards the masking of intuitive powers and creating cognitive dissonance between people and what they can experience with their own senses, which is another story for a different book. The one important caveat to trusting our instincts is that we should trust them to a lesser degree when we're under stress. Why? Because they're being contaminated by stress hormones that cloud our judgment, decisions, and reasoning.

In failing to understand how the hormones of stress can unleash a pharmaceutical storm of downers in your system, you can unwittingly have a harrowing morning commute turn into a day of poor decision-making. Also, unless you've done a lot of personal development work and healing from trauma, your ego's concerns and doubt can become mistaken for truth.

Additional factors may include a lack of nourishment and/or exercise, as well as other chemical issues that affect your brain and the homeostasis of your body. Based on your clarity, nutrition, relaxation, and so forth, only you can determine how accurately your radar is dialed from day to day.

Do you often wish you had followed an intuition, instinct, or gut feeling? If so, the next time it happens, I recommend writing down what that little voice is telling you exactly as it enters your mind. If your reaction to the concern is, *Oh, there's that fear coming up again,* then you might be dealing with an egoic concern or an old emotional wound that needs to be addressed in order to free yourself and grow beyond it. On the other hand, if you feel that what you've written is a sort of wake-up call, pay attention to it.

In the world of business, I greatly admire leaders who manage to stay happy and at peace with their businesses, even as they experience the usual ups, downs, turnarounds, and general uncertainty. The common thread that strings together this unique breed of entrepreneurs is that they've all put in the time, focus, and intention to develop and trust their instincts—which, when you are in tune with your body, actually manifest as a feeling in the gut. This feeling that comes from the "brain in your gut" is revolutionizing medicine's understanding of the links between digestion, mood, health, and even the way we think.[45]

Despite the fact that their decisions may go against the winds of popularity, great leaders know when to follow their gut. As a result, they might walk away from clients, candidates, deals, and anything they don't have a good feeling about. The chances are likely that when you're still in startup mode, you're not yet a master, but as time goes on, you will learn to distinguish when to listen to your intuition and when to disregard it.

The individuals among us who have the most observable deployment of instincts are athletes. As an example, in football, the offensive and defensive coordinators are always looking for body language, eye movement, and the telegraphing of other players at levels that are almost imperceptible. For instance, if a defensive lineman shifts his weight from one side to the other, the other team's coaches know that's the way he'll run. These observations are calculated consciously, and players are trained to recognize them as a prediction tool. When practiced enough, on the field, they become instinctual. This is all to say that while you already possess high-performance instincts, most of your business instincts are developed from playing the actual game, and to step onto the field and have fun with them is one of the most rewarding aspects of business ownership. The more you play with this guidance system, the more successful you'll become not only navigating challenges but staying ahead of them. And the more of a connection your team has to this wisdom, the greater their ability to operate without you having to be there.

In my experience, a strong female team leader's instincts are typically impeccable at timing important initiatives, for instance, strategy execution. When she thinks about it, that is the time to do it. Females more than males, it seems, can sense disturbances in the field (sometimes to a fault), and while there are theories, for now, this ability cannot be explained through science. As I said earlier, the US military is already deploying this unique capability of women in hostile environments.

I believe someday in the not too distant future, this connection with unseen patterns will be something humankind will take for granted, and in doing so, it will revolutionize consciousness. What all of this comes down to is neurobiology, connection to the field, and perception (or what has been called extrasensory perception). It's a topic I've been fascinated by for some time, and I am excited to see how the near-future discoveries in the fields of particle physics and awareness bring these factors to light.

The most important thing I can share about instincts is that to avoid the glass cliff in entrepreneurship you need the consistent courage to act on your gut, despite it being a thankless and risky undertaking. If you think, "I should go ahead and do that," *don't put it off*.

And then relax around the risk.

RELAX AROUND THE RISK

Make no mistake—starting a business is risky, which is why so many fail in the first year,[46] but sometimes it's not because people fail to plan, aren't smart enough to make it work, or the market rejects their idea. It's a lack of coherence or alignment within themselves. The simple fact of the matter is that if you're not committed to and aligned with your vision, you'll self-sabotage it. This applies to everyone from the CEO to the frontline worker.

It's for this reason that I always ask people who are thinking about entrepreneurship to do their homework by running budget models with real costs and cash outlays—as well as making sure the idea is aligned with your nonnegotiables (for example, having my child with me). Once you get started, if you hesitate or allow doubt to set in, you may hinder the venture—perhaps even permanently. *Don't be a waffler. Don't be wishy-washy.*

Regarding actual risk, I believe you can turn the odds in your favor with your intent and your desire. For instance, have you ever been 100 percent sure of your ability to do something that seemed impossible to others? Remember how that felt. This doesn't mean you won't feel a bit of trepidation or quite a lot of nervousness. I have always found that a bit of fear is right where you want to be. That's called your edge. The real fun, however, begins when you can transmute that fear into excitement.

Economies don't always expand, industries don't always grow, and disruptions happen. High-end earners always account for cycles and seasons. It's all part of the game. Your most formidable competitors are the ones who always play their operations and sales game like it's headed into an economic downturn. There's no fat in their chop, they're hungry for every deal, and they don't rest for long. They're prepared for the next cycles—cycles where weak or inefficient companies will suffer the most. Then they take advantage of the opportunity and claim market share. While others are cutting costs to survive, they use the extra capacity to retool, retrain, innovate, and recruit some amazing talent.

After I had my business for a couple of decades, I distinguished that the worst-case scenario was that I might have to live under a bridge and that this scenario had crept into my conscious mind as a longtime fear. After turning into a bit of a workaholic from working on a very risky project for about a year, and because the stakes were so high, this fear of losing everything became so pervasive in my subconscious that I once thought about giving everything away and actually living under a bridge for a few weeks to get over it. That year, four of my friends, plus my dog, died from cancer in a fourteen-month period. It was that year that I decided to live without fear and hesitation and to design a renewed purpose, which was to promote a CEO to take my place in the lodging company, write a book, and be a land developer. In doing so, I've never looked back. I chose to blast my fear into fierceness.

BLAST FEAR INTO FIERCENESS

When an IFL learns to transmute fear into fierceness, focus, and fortitude, the big, intense emotions she'll experience as a high-performance CEO aren't something she can plan for—but they're something she will learn to *thrust herself into*. The next time you feel highly emotional about a seemingly insurmountable challenge, perhaps even more so than feeling rational about it, I want you to think of the following analogy about a rocket.

The elements of thrusting a rocket into space require a super-concentrated focus of energy. In the case of your business launch, your *emotions* provide the energy for that liftoff. When our business is conceived, getting our emotions in line with our intention is the very first challenge, but at some point, there comes a time where we *just know we're going to make it happen*. At that point, it's our resolve to be unstoppable that provides the rocket fuel to get past the part of our brain called the *amygdala*, which exists to protect us by detecting and processing fear.[47]

This amygdala—being the prediction machine that it is—is designed to keep you from repeatedly hurting yourself. It will also block you from connecting with the infinite field of potential by redirecting your focus toward what can go wrong. What's worse, it can process information at lightning speed, and much of it occurs under your cognitive radar. Have you ever heard the saying that FEAR stands for False Evidence Appearing Real?

As founders of businesses, we typically don't get to ease into our business game. We don't spend much time sticking our toe in the water. We take a stand, and the people and circumstances in our lives have to organize around it—instead of us organizing around them. We set the trajectory by imagining that our outcome is already fulfilled, and with that end in mind, we create our blueprint. Then we focus exclusively on mission-critical tasks (both personal and professional) to reduce the drag coefficient. Without over-thinking it, we continue to yield to our highest outcome as being possible and attainable. *We make a choice—and then we launch into the unknown.*

Just like rocket scientists, we entrepreneurs must work within natural laws. And as those laws change beyond a certain point in the atmosphere of entrepreneurship (just as the laws change outside Earth's atmosphere), so too do they change *when you get beyond your mind's ability to predict or control things.* That's when your business takes off like a rocket, because suddenly you're faced with no gravity. To operate in the postlaunch environment of infinite possi-bility, we have to train our ego's need for predictability to stand aside and also give up the smaller personalities we once had. At this new altitude, the gravitational pull of your past doesn't even exist, except to provide wisdom, guidance, and trajectory.

Here, on the business side of your spiritual path, you'll get instant feedback about what you're creating. You can think of these as divine reflections that exist above and beyond the atmosphere of the collective consciousness. It's here, at this zero-gravity altitude, where an absence of archetypal feminine heroes doesn't even matter, that you'll create your life as a leader. And it's from this elevated perspective that you set the tone for all areas of your life.

CHAPTER 4

PLAY TO WIN

Because we're in a necessary era in our society of focusing on inclusion and being aware of one's privilege, talk of winning isn't trending right now. You might feel uncomfortable discussing how to win, lest you cause someone else to lose. However, just because a professional sports player has the skills to win games and earns $50 million a year doesn't mean he can't actively participate in efforts for societal equality, and the same goes for you. For anyone hustling and bringing all they've got to a game, winning feels as good as it looks—especially when you're playing against a *lesser version of yourself.*

Now that we have that disclaimer out of the way, let's talk about *you winning* as an Inspired Feminine Leader, which means whatever you want it to mean. To me, it means winning enough big projects to create a lot of well-paying jobs, have my mom's house paid for and my grandkids' college fund handled, and not have to look at prices of items at the grocery store. For you, it will be something unique *to you.*

Because you're an entrepreneur, it follows that you realize

that, like any game, your business has players, rules, goals, winners, and losers. The players are those of us who start business entities that are inherently worth nothing when they are conceived. At the outset, many of us incur considerable debts, and all of us take risks. *The outcomes of the game are simple:* winners get customers, earn market share, and to some degree, financial freedom. The losers pack up shop and look for another gig. No matter how inspired, how feminine, or how much of a leader you are, it's vital to acquire a taste for winning.

If you've never experienced winning or you've lost the taste for it (which happens), just start small and accrue incremental experiences of victories. Get a small win, then a bigger one, and then a bigger one. As Scott Barry Kaufman of the Imagination Institute in the Positive Psychology Center at the University of Pennsylvania states, "Small accomplishments can boost inspiration, setting off a productive and creative cycle." Kaufman goes on to say that "another, critically overlooked, trigger for inspiration is exposure to inspiring managers, role models, and heroes."[48] As you deploy your vision to lead your teams to small victories and turn every failure into a learning experience, you will see ever-increasing levels of creativity, problem-solving, and results.

If a competitive athlete wants to get better, she isn't going to play down a level. She plays with people who are better than she is because they elevate her game. If your team keeps playing in leagues that have better players, their game will continue to rise until, at some point, they surpass those competitors.

Just as coaches take time to develop their strategies and

talent pool throughout seasons, you will build a personal winning dynasty if you put all the elements in place in a committed, passionate, focused, and skillful fashion, whether your business is big or small. So, be proud of yourself for doing a good job and taking care of the client, and next, let's cover the fundamentals of where I see small to medium-sized companies drop the ball the most.

The tactics I describe for you below have been the force multipliers for high performance in both my business and my personal life, which means they allow me to stay supported in my quest to avoid burnout and stay engaged, inspired, and in my true function. *For me, that is winning.*

WINNING TACTIC #1: BUILD YOUR TEAM THE IFL WAY

To be inspired means to feel blessed, hopeful, and grateful. Therefore, to be an inspired leader, you must surround yourself with people who make you feel blessed, hopeful, and grateful instead of people who are there because of a paycheck. Finding and recruiting team members who have the potential to match your ability to create new revenue streams, serve clients, and create more jobs without the need for your constant oversight is key for IFLs.

Don't let anyone be indispensable to the game, especially you.

The caveat to replicating yourself, however, is to make sure you allow your team to complement your skills and close the gaps created by your weaknesses. After several decades of hiring, I find it's essential to learn to love real diversity among team members, because we perform better when we have a consortium of views, work styles, backgrounds, personalities, and outlooks. (I especially encourage you to place a high value on the contribution of introverted, detail-oriented individuals who don't require a ton of attention but have your and your clients' backs no matter what.)

Then, like a chess match, your job becomes figuring out what tasks to give the most effective teammates to dominate in the marketplace—*then* put *more* resources behind those individuals. As soon as financially possible, and especially during periods of growth, stack specialists in your most impactful positions two persons deep so that each role has someone who is shadowing or training, especially if their skills are complementary instead of exactly the same.

The best management decision we've ever made was to start using profile tools like the Culture Index (www.cindexinc.com). The Culture Index measures autonomy, sociability, multitask behavior, and attention to detail in a highly efficient way. This allows you to assess and identify what types of occupational DNA you're looking for in each role—and it does this with a label. My profile is called a "Rainmaker," which explains a lot. For instance, I'm the type of person who might write a million-dollar deal on a napkin...then lose the napkin.

As a result of my lack of attention to that level of detail, I have to recruit more detail-oriented profiles—such as administrators, specialists, or craftsmen—to handle every single file and folder, from contracts and checklists to my own bank statements, plans, procedures, and templates. Later in my career, I've also become relatively useless at any client-facing tasks other than sales and escalated customer service. I don't do client fulfillment (logistics and operations) in my corporate housing business anymore, but that's just my choice based on my skills and the needs of the business as it exists today.

Yes, you can and will do everything (aka be the chief cook *and* bottle washer) for a certain period, but why should you continue to do things that take you away from your primary functions? To handle such things, find brilliantly capable teammates who do it ten times better than you ever could. Having these complementary skills come together through the team brings homeostasis to the business organism.

As an example, let's look at accounting. Accounting and financial reporting are crucial for obvious reasons, but it's a reporting of the *past*. During our monthly budget-to-actual meetings, when our controller presents financial information that reflects what's in the rearview mirror, I have trouble not mentally drifting away. By nature, I prefer to "sense" what's occurring in the present rather than analyzing it.

Is this a weakness? Yes. A strength? *Also yes*.

As a business leader, you *must* be authentic about your areas of disinterest (or deficiency) and get them handled by someone while educating everyone on your team about your preferences. For example, I prefer our CFO to dig into the spreadsheets and trends to report his high-level findings rather than playing with the data myself. This might seem unusual for an owner of a business, unless you consider that the business, and all its processes, were designed around that owner.

WINNING TACTIC #2: HAVE A PROCESS FOR EVERYTHING

This sounds cliché, but there are frighteningly few companies in the small- to middle-market realm (with the exception of franchises) that have mastered this practice, and it comes with a massive cost in human capital and lost sales due to products and services not being delivered consistently.

One of the most influential books I read during my first year in business was written by Michael E. Gerber: *The E-Myth: Why Most Small Businesses Fail and What to Do about It*. The reason Mr. Gerber is considered by many to be the father of modern entrepreneurship is that he presented business founders such as myself with a very unfiltered version of the most common mistake a startup can make. That mistake, Gerber asserts, "is to fail to create replicable, scalable systems that anyone in your business can follow." In short, he said if you don't do so, you're not an entrepreneur. Instead, you're a "technician having an entrepreneurial seizure." I was fortunate enough to meet Mr. Gerber many years later, and I had the opportunity to thank him for his contributions to the world of small business owners.

The impact this book had on me was immense. As soon as I figured out how to perform even the smallest task in my new company, I turned it into a checklist as though I was going to have to use that checklist to show someone else how to do it. These checklists later came to be known as our standard operating procedures (SOPs), which everyone's business should have for anything at all that is to be done a certain way.

IFL-owned businesses *must* have SOPs for everything, or

you will spend a huge part of your week dealing with discrepancies in how things are handled, and your clients won't know what to expect from your company from one job to the next. If you don't create written processes, your best employees will become indispensable (and hold you hostage, in a sense) because there is no written document on how they do things. If they leave or get sick, there will be no one that can do it like they do. This weakens your company and puts a cap on growth.

Therefore, shortly after moving from concept to initializing your startup, and no matter how big or small you plan to grow, you should build systems, procedures, and checklists for:

- Production, service delivery, customer service
- Billing, handling payments, accounting, financial reports, budgeting
- Lead generation, converting leads, marketing, branding
- Recruiting, hiring, compensation plans, payroll, legal compliance
- Conflict resolution, root cause analysis, process improvement
- Performance reviews, coaching, performance improvement plans
- Sourcing suppliers, vendor management

Your business will have a *better chance* of surviving if you also have proactive systems in place (rather than being reactive) for:

- Appreciation and acknowledgment
- Employee satisfaction

- Skills development, advanced education and growth opportunities

And your business will *thrive* if you also have systems for:

- Measuring what causes sales
- Measuring customer satisfaction
- Management policies
- Team and culture building
- Performance-based compensation
- Breakthrough goals (covered later in this chapter)

Each of these systems can be codified into checklists for different scenarios and recorded into an online company directory. This becomes your living SOP manual.

My company has manuals that are regularly updated—especially when we have a customer-service mishap and subsequently perform a root cause analysis to determine the underlying process issue. So someone has to hold the priorities of working *on* the business and not just *in* the business. If you can't step away from serving clients, then you can't work *on* your business. Therefore, you need a stellar team around you to be able to do this.

In my experience, an IFL's process protocol is to (1) create the basic template for SOPs and (2) assign the employee who is the best at performing each task to write the first draft. Then you edit and proofread them, and lastly, put links to those SOPs into a training checklist for every role in the company, and have employees sign off on having been trained on them.

WINNING TACTIC #3: MAKE SALES AN INSIDE JOB

I can't write a chapter about being a business baller without talking about how IFLs bring in revenue. First, let's just say I have a very different attitude than most other CEOs: I think the best salespeople are made, not born. More than once, I've seen introverted, detail-obsessed customer service assistants turn into top-producing team leaders, outshining the company's sales veterans and so-called experts in the process. I've also seen a manager who said, "Please don't make me sell," win a President's Club award as the top salesperson.

A superstar salesperson is the individual on your team who is unstoppable in making the client happy. They don't have to look, sound, or act salesy. You don't even have to give them a title related to sales. Just ask them to call leads to find out what they need, and watch what happens.

You'll know when an employee is going to be worth their salt in helping you move money—they don't wait for additional training, better lead lists, fancy brochures, slick business cards, or a better website. Instead, they rabidly jump on the phone or get on planes to see your prospects and clients.

When you're fortunate enough to employ these types of nontraditional salespeople, you'll notice they are only passionate about one thing: *they work tirelessly for their clients—not for you.* When they're in the flow and making it rain for you and your clients in repetitive win-win scenarios, the hunt for the deal is like a drug, and there is no other drug like it. It's a high that is both enlivening and financially rewarding. They start to realize that competition can be intense, but that's just part of the game, not to mention a chance for them to bring their A game.

Although I was formally trained in selling the old-fashioned way, I have since let all those formulas go. My personal selling style is based on a mantra, or decree, that I created that I say to myself before I walk into every meeting. It goes something like this: "I make people successful, elevating their outcomes and their career (or their business), and I get paid for it." Then and only then, I match my intention to make the client successful with our offering. We have thrived on repeat business for twenty-five years doing things this way.

If you're a new or future CEO and don't have a sales background, do not worry. Regardless of whether you have experience, your ability to communicate your company's unique selling proposition will become second nature. What may not ever become second nature is the number of conversations you'll be having about it—which will start to feel awkward after the 1,021st time, but you have to *learn to love it* as the owner. This repetitive cheerleading activity (sales) is the only function, besides leadership, that you can't delegate at the beginning, and it should always be at the heart of your business.

One more thing: when facing competition in a sales setting, there is a thing called "sportsmanship." You should never trash your competition to a client. Besides making you look bad, you don't know the level of personal connection your competitor has with that client. Yes, there is psychological warfare waged by your opponents at times, but I recommend sticking to a defensive, rather than offensive, posture in that area (especially if you believe in karma). When my prospective clients bring up my competition, I simply say, "They're a great company, but our clients prefer us because we do things a little differently—for instance, we do x, y, and z—and that seems to really work for them."

When the sales game is played ethically, the only casualties should be points on the board and maybe a few financial or pride injuries for the loser. When a sale happens, jobs are created for the winner, and if done right, a good time is had by all.

As an IFL, remember that there are as many preferences in selling methods as there are salespeople in which to use them. That said, in my opinion there is no one-size-fits-all method for getting clients to buy, and thus there's no need for a sales department per se. Instead, *everyone is on the sales team*, even if you have certain people who are on a quota and others who aren't. Everyone gets paid bonuses on company results, even the accounting team. That's why I believe *everyone on the team* needs to find a method for connecting with customers and asking for more business that resonates with her unique style and use it whenever possible.

WINNING TACTIC #4: MANAGE, LEAD, OR GET OUT OF THE WAY

Ask yourself this question: Are you more of a manager or a leader at heart? Would you rather direct, assign, control, mitigate risk, plan details, and use your head? Or do you prefer to enroll, encourage, inspire, take risks, and use your heart? Do you enjoy focusing on how to maximize the bottom line or keep your eyes on the long-range vision?

Of course, you're probably a bit of a combination of these tendencies, but if you had to choose, which one would it be? It's important to know because it works better to have equal measures of management and leadership in your company. So it's very, very important to notice who the leaders are and who the managers are (including yourself) and promote or recruit accordingly in order to surround yourself with the requisite skills to accomplish what *doesn't* inspire you.

Personally, I am an *absentee* manager and a *hands-on* leader. Although I thoroughly enjoy creating systems, I get very turned off by inspecting people's work quality, tracking whether they're meeting deadlines, and training them on how to do tasks. On the other hand, I get totally fired up when it comes to recognizing process inefficiencies, sales opportunities, and strategy formulation, then creating plans to execute on these observations.

If you're more of a leader than a manager, consider getting help from your managers to create your set of management SOPs. I recommend checking into a *balanced scorecard* system, or something similar. Put your managers' goals on your calendar and have them present to you quarterly without fail. In the next section, I cover why it's important to focus on your management systems early and often.

WINNING TACTIC #5: THINK LIKE A PROSPEROUS VISIONARY

Whether you're a manager, a leader, or a combination, you probably have some of your systems and processes in place, while others need improvement (or don't yet exist). That's understandable. But here I want to give you further inspiration to consider the importance of your team creating, maintaining, and sustaining written processes and systems as it relates to winning the entrepreneurial game.

If you want to get to what I call in my wealth courses "a prosperous visionary role," at the very least, you'll want to examine the way you think about processes. In my company, every time we've let our processes slip, two things have happened: (1) people have started assuming that business just happens and have gotten very, very sloppy, and (2) I've had to roll up my sleeves and fix things that had been fixed multiple times before, which is maddening.

If you don't build systems and have your team maintain them (and upgrade as needed, of course), you run the risk of being what I call a "hardworking technician" instead of a CEO. Or worse, if you don't bring a systems mindset at all, your game might never even launch, and instead, you'll end up in the category of a *dreamy idealist*, a term I affectionately use to describe someone who's (sometimes permanently) in the dreaming phase of things.

To determine whether you're operating like a prosperous visionary, a hardworking technician, or the dreamy idealist, I created a quiz for you. Here are ten true-or-false questions to gain insight into your current thinking, followed by three simple exercises to improve your score. The more honest you are, the more helpful this exercise!

T/F	I spend at least as much time working *on* my business as *in* my business.
T/F	I am confident my product or service can sell because hundreds, thousands, or millions of individuals are already buying something like it in the marketplace, or it solves a problem no one has solved—that people do think is a problem.
T/F	My target market can easily understand my product without much explaining.
T/F	I can see clearly that as soon as I've launched my startup and it's profitable, we'll have a team and all the operating procedures required to take care of customers without me.
T/F	I have a concrete plan to scale my business beyond what I can handle personally in the next year. I will have systems and people to make the company perform without a lapse in service.
T/F	My clients and I are clear about what our competitive advantage is compared to other options.
T/F	Our loyal customers appreciate our offerings and call us when they need us.
T/F	We have a clear and distinct plan for generating repeat revenue throughout the year from some or most of our customers.
T/F	We regularly measure our income against expenses, pay our bills on time, and have a clear reporting system to know where we stand financially. We're selling products at a profit.
T/F	I have successfully run profitable projects and/or businesses in the past, with a profitable and happy ending for all involved.
TOTALS	True ____ False ____

Okay, let's figure out your score! How many did you answer in the affirmative?

0–3: You're either a lover of blue sky, or you're in the embryonic stage of thinking about your business. I encourage you to read up on business planning, hire a coach, go to business school, attend seminars, listen to webcasts, or read books about business ownership. Even before that, spend time talking to the business owners you admire and want to be like. Explore if this is what you really want to do.

4–7: Count yourself among the ranks of "high potential" entrepreneurs, and make sure you're always honing your CEO-ship skills. Unless you'd love to work with clients and employees on a committed and consistent schedule for the foreseeable future, you'll really want to focus on building an enterprise rather than working so hard.

8–10: A potential rock star, if you're not already one! You wouldn't have gotten this far without valuing continuous improvement and development. Now it's time to push your hard-won wisdom into your organization for your future leaders. Who needs mentorship and is part of your succession plan? Teach them now how to think like an owner. You'll end up at a whole new frequency and level of wealth when you have a team that can think like you.

Don't worry. If you're thinking like a dreamy idealist, it doesn't mean you can't learn to play the game. Also, there is nothing wrong with being a hardworking technician. I have brilliant, talented CEO friends who earn a great living but could never let go of client-facing activities because either they love what they do or they think they're the only ones who could do what they do. There's always someone who can do what you do, and if you think otherwise, you're just putting a ceiling on your income and committing yourself to indefinitely long workweeks that can turn into years. There's nothing at all wrong with that, but if you'd instead prefer to reach the role of a prosperous (aka wealthy) visionary someday, you have to find people who are better than you and trust them to take the reins.

WINNING TACTIC #6: COMMIT TO HAVING BREAKTHROUGHS

"One sentence," I said.

Our global account executive looked amazed, which is how I needed her to look.

"Okay, I'll bite," she said. "What one-sentence strategic plan are you proposing?"

It was early January, and although we still needed to flesh out our plan for that year, I'd asked her to come to my house alone without the rest of the executive team. I reasoned that she was the only individual who would be open to my unfathomable, unthinkable goal, and she was also our top salesperson the year before.

"I want us to be the largest lodging company in Texas."

She took a breath, absorbing the gravity of the vision. She'd been around the process of setting and achieving break-through goals before.

"Let's do it," she said.

We made zero friends when we returned to the office and announced the plan, even among the executives who had helped break company records in the past. I told them that because we hadn't met our goals the prior year, or the year before that, we needed to do something radically different. My partner in crime and I explained how we would implement the plan, which involved opening multiple new business units in which we had no experience.

That single-sentence strategic plan tripled our revenues and was fully executed within five months. In the process, we became the state's largest temporary-lodging provider and the country's seventh largest. Because we had to innovate an entirely new way of delivering lodging services, I had requests from developers all over the country to meet and see how we were doing things. I finally started charging $5,000 for a meeting (which was, of course, applied to their fees if they selected us as a project partner).

It was an excruciatingly intense period of rapid growth in a market that was brand-new to everyone (the newly discovered oil shales of South Texas), and we had not two but three new product lines being implemented in a single quarter. In hindsight, the company would have perished had we not created these new lines, even though there were days when some of us wanted to slap a bitch upside the head.

It took a while for us to recover from this "win" in terms of corporate culture, alignment, and stability. We went through three controllers in one year, and I experienced two significant betrayals within eighteen months. When money is flying in the door, you give people tons of autonomy and responsibility, and if you hire too fast and give those new hires too much power, you're asking for trouble. Since then, we've added management procedures that didn't exist and recruiting processes that better protected us for another massive growth surge several years later.

But setting and meeting that breakthrough goal was nothing short of a miracle. By aligning around that goal, we diversified our product offerings, promoted people to higher levels of responsibility and compensation, and became a company that eats problems for breakfast and sh*ts them out by lunch. A breakthrough goal is never about just making a number. It's about who your team members have to become (and what your organization has to become) to make that number happen.

Of course, all competent CEOs schedule goal-setting meetings at predictable intervals to align employees. There's just one caveat. If you set goals that are too easy, in my experience, you and your team will go into sleep mode, thus being far *less likely to accomplish them*. When my company sets a goal for mild improvement from one year to the next (say, 10 percent growth), we rarely achieve it. Yet every year that we create goals that we have no idea how to meet (aka breakthrough goals), we're more likely to outperform ourselves.

My team is fascinated by this phenomenon. I've seen breakthrough goal-setting create miraculous outcomes many times but didn't understand the mechanics behind it until I started my meditation practice. The reason for setting breakthrough-level goals is that when a team aligns around that type of lofty goal, they go through the conscious action of *choosing* it, despite the path being unknown. To *choose* it, they have to *align* with it—even though they'll have to get outside their paradigm to cause it. To *align* with it, they must *give themselves permission* for it to manifest and, in doing so, imagine what it will be like to accomplish that goal. This is the same process I go through when I activate new potentials in my life through the concentrated focus of meditation.

WINNING TACTIC #7: OBSERVE THE POWER OF AGREEMENTS

After running four businesses and coaching hundreds more, in my opinion, the primary difference between an ordinary business and an extraordinary business is the quality of the agreements. That's why it's vitally important to know what they are, why they're important, and how to use them.

Your life is already created by a set of agreements, whether conscious or unconscious, spoken or unspoken, clear or unclear. They're adopted from our relatives, culture, education, and so on. Observing the specificity (and also the directness, if you will) of your agreements with people is a fascinating exploration into how they set the foundation for every aspect of your life.

Sloppy agreements lead to unfulfilled desires and unmet expectations, and when left unchecked, slowly fray the fibers that support our vitality and hold our relationships together. Within society, the result is self-pity and narcissism, which cripples our happiness, productivity, sense of purpose, and even our health.

On the other hand, intentionally cocreating clear agreements at work and home sets a powerful context for specific areas. Otherwise, the contexts are dictated by arising circumstances. That kind of reactionary behavior born out of disappointment, fear, or anxiety causes people to control, manipulate, or maneuver those circumstances until they finally destroy all possibilities for collaboration. While I know it sounds conceptual, check out the patterns in this table, as I've seen this play out repeatedly with human beings:

CLEAR AGREEMENT =	UNCONSCIOUS EXPECTATION =
Clear context for the agreement	Unmet desire
+	+
Decisive boundaries around expectations	Disappointment, judgment, resentment
+	+
Predictability based on alignment to a context	Damaged relationships
	+
+	Confusion, passive aggression, doubt, quitting, pain
Ability to create because expectations are met	
	+
+	Difficulties collaborating in the future
Possibility for future mutual agreements	

My question to you then is: Are your agreements—which are creating the context for your life—working for you or against you? If you have consistent unmet expectations anywhere in your life, you probably haven't made them clear. I'm most passionate about this topic in the area of parent-child relationships. If you learn to establish clear agreements early and often with your kids, when they become teenagers, you'll have a strong foundation of respect, honor, and integrity in which to deal with them.

What if you took inventory of your most authentic desires in your key relationships, both personal and professional, and communicated them easily and joyfully? Then, what if you *co-created* clear agreements to support everyone's mutual highest outcomes? The result is a wholly upgraded model for relating to people with a new shared trajectory for creativity, fulfillment, and happiness. Here are some examples I suggested to a consulting client who had zero experience with clear agreements:

1. We agree to be punctual to meetings and leave our phones back at our desk.
2. We agree to wait until someone is finished speaking to share our information.
3. We agree to use a timer when succinctness is essential and multiple people need to speak or share ideas, and we agree each person will get x amount of time for their topic.
4. We agree to leave gossip at home and run our company with authentic, open communication (including feedback) and to eliminate all unnecessary complaints.
5. We agree to allow people to forgo after-hours company events with no penalty and no questions asked, assuming it's for the best in balancing their priorities.
6. We agree to schedule company events during business hours so everyone can participate.
7. We agree to bring our concerns to someone who can do something about it and, as a follow-up, place these concerns in writing.
8. We agree not to vent (complain or make toxic statements) for the sake of venting.
9. We agree to allow x amount of unpaid leave per year for team members who need extra time off for personal reasons, so long as the workload can be handled, and we agree temporary labor will be brought in if required.
10. We agree to say when we don't feel aligned with a strategy even if we agree with it in principle. We also agree

to align with a plan that has been decided even if we don't agree with it. (Example: the new office hours are starting thirty minutes earlier, and you now get one hour for lunch instead of thirty minutes.)

I recommend having a dialogue and reviewing your current agreements—including written, unwritten, spoken, or unspoken—with your executive team members. It would also be beneficial to put these agreements in your annual company reviews or strategic plan, because by cocreating new agreements regularly and/or every time you feel things slipping into familiarity, you'll cause mutually assured higher outcomes.

To the extent we live in a free society, you always have a choice to enter into an agreement. The ones that feel wrong to you are the ones you should renegotiate. Examples:

- "Joe, I'd like to renegotiate our agreement to present the report to our stockholders by the end of the month. Would it be possible to send it out on the first Friday of the following month?"
- "Kids, I'd like to renegotiate our plans on Saturday. I'm exhausted from work, and I'd like to pick something more low-key than the amusement park. We will reschedule Six Flags within the next month."

If you look closely, the agreements we *consciously* make are actually all with ourselves. When I have a conversation with someone and give my word with regard to a specific outcome or action, I'm not only making a promise to them; I'm committing to myself. If I break my agreement, I should be viewing it as being out of alignment not only with whom

I had the agreement but, perhaps more importantly, with myself.

The question you need to ask yourself then is, Why am I breaking this agreement? It's because I'm not aligned. Therefore, people whom you allow to break their word consistently are showing you the lack of alignment either in your system or in yourself.

Here's an example of a conversation I might have with a consulting client, asking him to describe how the new, clear agreements are playing out for him and his business partner:

> Me: Hey, Joel, how are your agreements with Judy going?
>
> Joel: Terrible. She already broke two of the three we created earlier this month. I cannot tolerate this lack of accountability any longer.
>
> Me: Wow. It sounds like you're not accountable to yourself.
>
> Joel: What?
>
> Me: Why are you choosing to blame Judy for you not being accountable for yourself?
>
> Joel: I hate being put in the position of enforcing the logical consequences of *her* broken agreements. Why should I have to? This always seems to happen to me!
>
> Me: You don't *have* to. But if you choose to, this lack of

workability will cease, and you'll be more likely to stop the persistent pattern throughout your life altogether. Is it clear to you what to do?

Joel: Yes, I have to offer to buy her out or sell my part of the business to her. And I need an iron-clad, written contract with her because there is no way I can work with a partner who doesn't keep her agreements.

Me: What will you do next time?

Joel: Next time, I will perform my due diligence, so before jumping into a partnership, I can be clearer about a partner's commitment and track record.

Me: Excellent! How do you feel?

Joel: Smarter, more empowered, but dreading my conversation with Judy.

Me: You're letting go of a belief about yourself in order to have this conversation. What is that belief?

Joel: That I don't deserve support.

Me: Have you let it go?

Joel: Yes!

To review: *Anyone who's repetitively breaking clear agreements with you is giving you a reflection of a broken agreement you have with yourself.*

Don't ever undertake a project—with anyone—without getting everything in writing in advance. If someone says you can write it later, say, "No, we can't." If they tell you that you're unreasonable, you can say, "I have to write the memo now, and we can adjust it later, or I'll forget what we said." Then have an attorney look to see if there's any chance of confusion or omissions.

The rules of engagement have to be precise. Every. Single. Time.

Where client lists and proprietary information aren't involved, I sometimes deploy a simple memo of understanding, which clearly states what each party understands as the agreement. People sometimes have a weakness for holding those they love (such as project partners) to a previous agreement. It's a buzzkill to press pause on a lovefest to place in writing what each party is responsible for. It can at first seem like it's removing the mystery and excitement, but in the long term, it really helps avoid any confusion or conflict. This is actually a great thing, for it keeps the train, the conductor, the engineer, and the passengers all rollin' on down the tracks.

Another reason people don't want to put things in writing is that they're actually not clear on what they want. Not being able to put your agreement in writing because you don't know what to say implies a lack of clarity, and if you're not clear enough to agree to something, *don't do it*. I can tell you from experience, this type of story does not have a happy ending and creates big distractions in business. Unclear agreements are especially rampant in small businesses, less so in middle-market businesses, and rare in big corporations. That should tell you something.

Through countless conversations, I've seen that many women have clear agreements in their personal lives but lack them in business. I have girlfriends who won't date a man seriously if he doesn't follow specific protocols, but these very same women will veer completely off course in their careers (without realizing it) due to not having clear agreements with clients, bosses, or employees.

Masculine figures, on the other hand, might be more prone to be masters of clear agreements in business but refuse to make them in their personal lives. (Whoops! There I go again making sweeping generalizations. Please forgive me for what I have observed.)

Before we move on, if you like, take a few moments to reflect on these questions:

- What suffering is occurring in your organization with an employee, a client, or a vendor?
- Where is there not a clear agreement in that situation?

After you carefully examine where or what the specific lack of clarity is, schedule a conversation to express how you noticed the two of you might be missing some clarity in your prior agreements. Tell them how you would love to align and clear up the misunderstandings to get both of you unstuck or clear.

On a final note, if someone resists making clear agreements with you, don't do business with them. They will quickly demonstrate to you why their lives are a hot mess.

WINNING TACTIC #8: HAVE FUN WITH ACCOUNTABILITY

"How did you cause your team to fail?" the CEO asked the VP.

"I lost track of the numbers. I took my attention off of them," she replied.

In most other companies, you'd hear this VP making excuses. Perhaps she would have talked about a slowdown in the territory or thrown another department under the bus. She might have slipped in a comment about a lack of training for her team or gained sympathy for a death in her family. Believe me, when it comes to people spewing garbage as to the cause of why they didn't meet sales goals, I've heard it all.

As a business owner, you *must not* fall into this very human trap. If you avoid it, you'll be more effective than most humans occupying leadership positions. Even though we leaders can get as lazy as any mere mortal, we remain *100 percent responsible for what happens*, and the sooner you realize this, the sooner you'll reclaim your power—in any situation. In regard to how I might be the cause of not getting the results I desire, I've noticed I can't effectively hold teams accountable unless I also hold my own feet to the fire. As a leader, it's where your power lies. *The buck stops with you.*

The good news is you can absolutely have a good time with this. It might seem counterintuitive, but your sense of total responsibility will inspire people, including their ownership over everything you have delegated, abdicated, forgotten about, or cannot control. I've found that when the team knows they will never be blamed directly, because ultimately you presided over everything that happened, they will do things for you that they wouldn't do for themselves. They will pitch in at an unimaginable level to help you avoid getting burned, and that's because they are loyal and empowered.

Accountability consists of three main components, and all effective teams (run by CEOs who don't have to micromanage their people) contain these elements:

1. Mission, vision, values, and goals are clearly articulated and understood.
2. Overall plan (with allowances for course correction) and midterm deliverables are agreed upon and committed to.
3. Progress is measured, feedback is incorporated, and reward is based on results.

Beyond passion and leadership, the only way to make accountability more glamorous is to make things more exciting and challenging for your teams, as opposed to them just checking off tasks on a job requirement description. We always add "icing on the cake" benefits, like smaller interim games that are part of the larger game. This can include spot bonuses, recognition programs, and company events or recognitions for the completion of arduous tasks or impactful projects. These are all additional positive reinforcements, and if you have the right leadership and hiring systems in place, you'll rarely have to use negative reinforcement.

As a CEO, accountability isn't a one-and-done chore for you. Unfortunately, it has about the shelf life of a gallon of milk. But there's a hard way and an easy way to create patterns that support momentum in accountability. The hard way is by being a driven, workaholic, control-freak CEO who never takes her hands off the levers. She tends to play favorites with individuals who do the same, and—*voilà!*—a culture of overwork is born.

The easy way to counter this is by cultivating a great set of managers or directors who have a strong ability to train others in a constantly improving set of standard operating procedures. Relying exclusively on rock-star talent and sheer momentum will carry you for a while. Still, in the long run, it will be more exhausting than leading and managing the entirety of your employees to a particular vision, even if it sometimes rubs people the wrong way.

In either case, if the shared sales and operating vision is not articulated and enforced in every corner, your company is like a boat with a leak, and you're going to be in trouble. Even your executive team will let strategic plan deliverables fall by the wayside, for no other reason than "out of sight, out of mind." Thus, you need constant and consistent measurements that align to your strategic plan.

Think of your strategic plan as a professor's syllabus for the year. This is a map that leads you through what you need to accomplish by the end of the year. Since your employees signed up for the job, they're responsible for doing the work so you can all arrive at the same place together, but in the end, they're receiving a paycheck or bonuses rather than a diploma. To keep them on track, you have to make sure they're receiving information as to how they are doing.

This will allow you to work *on* the business rather than *in* it. After all, that's what *you're* accountable for, and this is what Inspired Feminine Leaders do.

WINNING TACTIC #9: ACKNOWLEDGE AND APPRECIATE

Another IFL winning method is showing appreciation in a very particular way.

The secret sauce of connecting with any human is to acknowledge them. Unfortunately, the word *acknowledgment* has somehow been co-opted to mean "compliment," even though there is a massively impactful difference between a compliment and an acknowledgment.

Here is the definition of *acknowledgment*:

- Recognition of the existence or truth of something
- An expression of appreciation

As these definitions clearly imply, when you acknowledge someone, you are recognizing the existence of a certain truth about something. For example, when someone completes a difficult task, you say, "You completed [name that difficult task]!" You do not say, "Wow, you're amazing," unless you want to compliment them instead of acknowledging them.

To me, it's crazy how so many executives get this wrong, yet it's a crucial part of your CEO repertoire. By deploying a simple two-step process, more than any other management tool I've seen, you can unlock people's brilliance by using (1) a specific type of acknowledgment and (2) a follow-up expression of appreciation.

A compliment makes someone feel like a fraud. Imagine the mind of one of your team members after you tell them they're amazing:

- "I'm amazing? She's just saying that."
- "She said I'm amazing because I did that. I wonder what she thinks about me the rest of the time."
- "It wasn't amazing. I was doing my job. What a drama queen."

On the other hand, if you say, "You finished that daunting task on time and under budget," the employee would understandably think:

- "She noticed that I did that thing on time and under budget. Wow, she's paying attention to my effort."
- "I feel seen right now."
- "Yep! I sure did!"

The point is, no one is ever going to say, "Yes, thanks for recognizing that I'm amazing." You might as well be complimenting someone on the color of their shirt.

Therefore, acknowledgment for what someone did, as well as its positive impact, simultaneously lifts the suffering of being misunderstood and not being seen. You'll stop wasting your precious energy and squandering their valuable time by no longer issuing lazy kudos.

WINNING TACTIC #10: CELEBRATE

Earlier, when I spoke about self-care as an antidote to pressure, I was talking about you as an individual. The organizational version of self-care, in my opinion, is celebration. And it deserves a mention as a phenomenal way to alleviate pressure in your company.

As I've mentioned, I've been blessed with the opportunity to perform coaching with groups and individuals to observe what makes people tick. Turning on their creative passion and amplifying it always made me feel like I was gaining more than I was giving. In my classes, the most profound result participants consistently reported came from an imagination exercise I required everyone to do, the result of which would bring them face-to-face with their highest imagined outcome.

The question that always prompted this profound moment was, "Now that you've achieved [insert your achievement], what's new and different in your world?"

The answer to this question was the same, *every...single... time...*whether the exercise involved a group or an individual, or whether I changed the script when I delivered it. They talked about being surrounded by friends and family, partaking in great meals or parties, smiling and conversing with those whom they love.

After leading so many of these imagination activation exercises, I came to understand that authentic celebration is a *very high state of being.* Most people know the difference between a real celebration and just another excuse to eat cake, drink booze, and hand out silly prizes. What I'm talking about is a joyful, heart-opening, momentous occasion in which genuine appreciation is flowing. And it is especially important after periods of sustained pressure.

If you want a culture of not only accomplishment but fulfillment, remember to refine your celebration skills as a leader. Also remember that the main ingredient isn't money, food, drinks, or applause, but *appreciation*. Likewise, appreciation is the foundation of gratefulness, satisfaction, and love. And that's what great leaders inspire and create.

WINNING TACTIC #11: PLAY "LIKE A GIRL"

Because I'm launching into some stereotypes in this section for the purpose of making a point, I'd like to note that I once gave a rather fiery speech to my undergraduate communications class (the underlying theory of which was informed by my women's studies professor the semester before), and in this speech, I ripped the consumer goods industry to shreds for what I asserted was "an industry-wide conspiracy to subtly perpetuate women in gender-stereotypical roles, some forty years after the feminist movement."

Specifically, there was a commercial at the time for Tide laundry soap that called anyone who switched to another brand a "Tide drop-out." The commercials showed a series of women who were having issues with the outcome of their husbands' work shirts. There was never a man doing laundry. Only women. And of course, cleaning-product branding managers continue to this day to perpetuate the stereotype that women are responsible for cleaning.

As a more mature adult, I've come to realize that cleaning products, like power tools, are purchased by one gender at least a little bit more than the other. I remembered that regardless of the justice of the situation, marketers are compelled to market to the decision-maker of a household, and that decision-maker is more often female for cleaning products. All of this is to say that it's possible I'm about to trigger some of my readers, but what I hope to accomplish is that you experience more inspiration and less stress, and kick some ass on the game field as a result of what I've written.

Based on my own observations and studying the subject of femininity, I would say the odds are strong that you, as a feminine leader, possess a certain set of gender-based talents and natural strengths that you may not even realize are in your arsenal in order to leverage them more. Here, I want to point out the strengths I've noticed in hundreds of women, and some of the men, who have access to their feminine energy. See if you relate to these:

1. *You can sense information (and energy) from multiple sources simultaneously, including from outside the room in which you're sitting.* In addition to having a sixth sense like any human, women are hardwired to take care of multiple children of different ages and abilities, while getting countless tasks accomplished. This translates to a certain degree of clairvoyance and/or clairsentience, which are huge boosts to business leadership.
2. *You can easily see the complexity of an issue, perhaps faster than others, and without even giving it much thought.* You instantly see what could go wrong, what could go right, who's on board with a proposed action and who hates it, and all the possible steps to achieve the outcome. This *ability to see*, which I call "radar" throughout the book, will be a huge asset to your team.
3. *You can persuade people (in an informal, conversational way) of what's most important to focus on and what they should all be doing.* Women are adept at shooting down

dumb ideas as effortlessly as a lit match turns a stack of papers into fire. Feminine leaders can also put very persistent earworms in your brain about what you're capable of doing, which will stretch you past your limits.

4. *You can touch people's hearts with a single statement or question because of the way you see things.* As a feminine leader, the fact that you can see the soft underbelly of almost every human being's ego will help you in creating a loving atmosphere in your company.

5. *You have an inclusive, holistic viewpoint, even if you don't always act on it.* You see the entire ecosystem and cannot compartmentalize, silo, or ignore it away. Even if you press on with a decision that seems insensitive to certain factors or people, you're somehow able to take the holistic view into account more readily than most. This results in stabler employee morale over the long term.

6. *You innately know how to run a family system.* A business is a family system because there are different ages, roles, abilities, hierarchies, formal and informal connections, outside obligations, internal needs, and emotional, intellectual, and physical (space) needs. You spend more time with coworkers than with families during waking hours, and women can roll with the close quarters quite easily.

7. *You're loyal, and it's personal that you're loyal.* People say we shouldn't make things personal, but when someone you care for at work needs help, you'll always empower them. Women develop working friendships and alliances that are as strong as any military squadron. When we're loyal to our team, and one of our coworkers gets hurt, we feel the hurt. When they win, we feel their win.

8. *You're grateful.* And gratitude means you give yourself permission to receive blessings, miracles, windfalls, and success, *right?*

By deploying your most innate strengths as your winning edge, you'll sustain yourself beyond setbacks, periods where you lack motivation, and times when the other parts of your life require more attention than your business. Once you put these winning tactics in place, there's a formula to make them part of a winning strategy. That formula is called *setting the tone.*

CHAPTER 5

SET THE TONE

When I tell people that I've worked an average of ten hours per week (sometimes way more, and most often less) for the past fifteen years in my company, they look at me with disbelief. As a matter of fact, I didn't want to tell you at the beginning of the book that this was the case because I didn't want to lose credibility with my readers.

The fact is, if you build the right team and set the right tone, *especially* during times of organizational stress, you can do whatever you want with the rest of your time. (I raised three kids, traveled for months per year, and started four other businesses with my extra time.) In the following sections, we explore how to level up your abilities in creating a context for exponential results while working fewer hours.

The first order of business is not to shy away from setting the tone in spite of your concerns for how you might be perceived. From an outsider's perspective, IFLs who are living in high performance might be unfairly interpreted as aloof or blunt in our communication styles—because of the double standard in which women are expected to watch our tone. But what may elude the casual observer is that the tone of a high-performance game isn't personal—it's *transpersonal*. While the tone in my company is nearly always friendly and respectful, at certain times, we express the raw, authentic emotion derived from our passion for putting points on the scoreboard.

By going from winning to losing and back again, my company has been forged like steel, boosting our organizational immune system and our people's resolve. To build that type of resilience, it's better to test your mettle on short-term, preferably self-induced circumstances, like outrageous goals. This resiliency and the ability to get through struggle intact is one of the most important pillars of fortifying the strength of your company.

BUILD COMPANY CULTURE

Company culture is defined as the beliefs and behaviors that determine how a company's employees and management engage with each other—plus how the company handles customers and suppliers. Sometimes, culture isn't written or defined; rather, it's implied. It can change over time, especially if you don't create systems to keep the original culture intact.

The reason your company's culture is crucially important is that it is like a hologram in which each individual embodies the parts of the whole. It's the *spirit* of the company, and the only way to have a great culture is to create one. I can't tell you what culture will serve your customers best and make you the happiest, but I can tell you with certainty that from the beginning, you should be unrelenting about creating your culture. If you don't, it will end up being a cesspool of dysfunction.

The best way to build a culture in a new company is first to observe the spirit of the founder(s) and try to express that spirit in words. (If "spirit" doesn't resonate with you, feel free to use "vision.") Secondly, you'll want to define the three or four ingredients that, mixed together, will make your customers happy. Sometimes, these are expressed as values, but to express them as such is not required.

When you add these factors together, you'll have a good start for cultivating your company's culture. Allow me to express it as an equation so you can plug in the values, preferably using the simplest of terms. Add these two items to make a sentence about your company:

Culture = Spirit of the founder(s) + What your customers have come to expect from your team

The spirit of my company is "adapting to ever-changing needs, demands, and opportunities." Anyone who knows me would say, "Yep, that's definitely Mandy's spirit." To build the culture of my company, we added that spirit to the things our clients expect, which are velocity, impeccability, high-energy, and being solutions-oriented. To describe our culture, I would paraphrase all these elements in the following statement: "Our company provides customized solutions with speed, accuracy, and enthusiasm."

Now that you know how to define your culture as it naturally unfolds, you can better set the tone by managing actions and policies that align with your culture and avoid those practices that go against it, including what goes into your standard operating procedures, employee manuals, and other things, such as marketing materials. This will also enable you to make hiring choices to support your culture, which dictates everything from your employment ads to your interview questions. When new team members arrive on the scene their first day of work, they should have already been indoctrinated during the interview process as to what attitude will be expected of them.

Last but not least, your reward systems should be tailored to reinforce the elements of your culture. In my company, we have peer-voted quarterly awards with gift certificates. These awards recognize team members who embody the elements that make our culture inseparable from what our clients depend on us for.

CONTROL THE NARRATIVE

The reason that setting the tone is the most powerful leverage you have is because *context is ten times more powerful than content*. As an IFL, the most important two things to remember in setting the tone are: (1) the *stories* create the context, and (2) *repetition* is your best friend because context has a short shelf life.

In spite of systems, procedures, and metrics, what really creates the intelligence of an organization are legendary stories. The most obvious benefit to effective storytelling is to make change management easier. When I learned how powerful stories can be, I nearly stopped sending company memos about important changes. I found out the hard way that it's difficult to include enough data to overpower the stories people make up about big change unless I replace that story with a better (truthful) one. Thus, I developed a strategy whereby I would first discuss with a few key people an upcoming decision, the aspects of the decision I was weighing, why I cared about it, and the reasons (story) for why I was leaning toward making it. I would then get their preliminary feedback.

While some would keep my musings to themselves, I knew others would not, which is what I was counting on. Then, in a very nonthreatening way, I would informally announce the likelihood of the change, along with a story about why I was considering it, to the entire team. The benefits of doing things this way included the elicitation of feedback through an informal network of communication, which paradoxically allows more control of the boundaries of the narrative.

While stories are important for controlling the narrative, repetition is even more crucial. I can't stress this enough: you *must* sound like a broken record when it comes to communicating the vision for all areas of your business. Even if your team helped you come up with that vision or did it themselves, they won't remember it in the heat of the game. As a leader, let one of your absolute greatest tools be repetition, even if you expertly find 1,001 ways to express the exact same thing.

Every conversation you have, whether one-on-one with an employee or in front of your whole company, is like a neuron firing, and according to Hebbian theory, neurons that fire together wire together.[49] Repetitive conversations in your business build the neural grooves of your company, just like repetitive tasks or actions build the neural networks in our brains.

My team still enjoys hearing sales stories from the early days, how we overcame adversity, outplayed our competitors, and so forth. The most effective ones are the micro stories regarding how current procedures came to be, how business models were born out of necessity, or what conditions were like on certain projects. These stories are legends, and they help new employees gain a long-range context for everything that's happening, besides letting them know you are also paying attention to the legendary things that are happening *now* from your visionary role.

One of the biggest strengths of an IFL is that she innately knows how to make it her mission to build the stories that make a positive difference and can effectively destroy the ones that victimize, blame, or complain. One of the ways we do this is through bringing consciousness to our own language, which is covered in the next section.

SPEAK CONSCIOUSLY: THE LANGUAGE OF CREATION

If I could change a single thing on planet Earth, it would be the way leaders speak and engage groups of people with words. The year I completed my conscious-language-instructor training, I felt like I had opened the doors to another dimension. The practice sessions at the end of our training caused me to have such mystical experiences that I forever saw the world differently. What happened to me after seven days of speaking impeccably is beyond what I'm willing to go into detail about in this book (like experiencing enhanced visual perception due to going from "particle" to "wave" consciousness). In summary, these very experiential trainings offered the three following takeaways:

1. Treat everything you say as a sacred prayer, especially when you say something with a charge or heightened emotion (whether positive or negative).
2. Know that your words are an instruction to your subconscious mind, so become more intentional about what you say and think.
3. Personal change occurs when a change in your energy occurs. This change in energy happens at a *choice point*. When your choice is made with heightened emotions, such as joy or enthusiasm (or safety and trust), the result is a transmutation of thoughts like "I can't..." into "*I can...*" or from "I don't have..." into "*Now that I have...*" and so on.

Again, the key is to generate with your attention a change of energy by deploying language—with feeling—toward what you choose to be, have, create, or enjoy rather than what you don't want, which is what people tend to focus on. It's liberating when you start to notice that you've attracted and manifested the aspects of your life according to the path of your dominant thoughts (aka your prayers and subconscious instructions). This is how you control the narrative.

CONSENSUS VERSUS COMMANDS

As a feminine entrepreneur, you probably realize that as women, we are rather hardwired to fit in, so we sometimes relinquish our command to a group ideology. In the realm of leadership, this is called abdicating. This feminine trait of being yielding can make even the most powerful women abdicate power to someone else's vision to avoid conflict, and it often comes back to bite them in the butt. This is why I constantly ask for agreement and feedback on my company's direction.

Sometimes it makes my instructions sound like suggestions, but the by-product is that people feel safe to tell me what isn't working. This is a good thing—you want to have a team that gives you something to push up against, lest you fall from your own gravity. When it comes to my executive team, if I'm facing the task of implementing an unpopular direction, I pick up the phone and call an advisor to bounce things off of. Because if I wait until I feel at peace with it, the indecision will lead to pressure, self-doubt, and distraction. (PS: It's never an accident which advisor you ask. You will usually get the exact advice you subconsciously know you need to hear, depending on whom you call.)

To make things easier around building consensus, when implementing plans or policies, invest time in appealing to your team members' vision of where they want to be in their future and set your company goals to align with the goals of your team. You would never, ever hear this counterintuitive policy being implemented in a big corporation, but I've found it's more profitable over the long run to convert your people to a shared vision than to coerce them.

On the other hand, I find that sometimes people actually want to be commanded. The intensity really lights people up, as long as it doesn't pressure them. I work best with people who can take the intensity and can also give it back to me. Why? Because that tells me both parties are passionate about coming to a solution for a challenge.

I had a vice president who would say to me, "I think you're wrong." He wouldn't wait until I was finished talking or send me a letter an hour later or ruminate about it for days. Instead, he went straight to the point so we could arrive at solutions faster—and as we all know, in business, speed counts. What made him a dependable and reliable person to work with was that if he was wrong, he would walk into my office and say so. Because we were so self-correcting, we could be intense with each other. To reiterate, it was *transpersonal*, not personal.

If you have a hard time giving commands, just think of major league sports, where losses are always the coaches' fault. Remember this when you're trying to choose between gaining consensus or giving a simple command: getting everyone's agreement doesn't mean it's a good decision, and if the team is completely wrong, *it's your fault anyway*.

You'll experience great freedom in the dynamic balance between consensus and command if you don't think in terms of right and wrong. Don't be paralyzed from making quick decisions that only have to be exactly right a percentage of the time. Think in terms of playing with the best information you have at each moment. It's a game, remember?

If knowing it's okay to be wrong isn't enough to enroll you in giving commands when they would do better than getting consensus, consider how it will impact your masculine employees.

My son was an NCAA Division I football athlete who played offensive line. Compared to most other players whom he went up against in his position, he lacked their beefy stature—young men who weighed more than three hundred pounds and who could squat more than seven hundred pounds, while also being able to run fifty meters in less than six seconds. For more than three hours every game day, his opponents tried to pancake him (knock him backward) in front of a crowd of more than fifty thousand people. Spectators stomped, screamed their lungs out at the players, and booed the referees, and their blood pressures visibly rose. *This is a man's idea of play.*

Masculine leaders dress up nicely and act civilized, but never forget that for them, business is a ruthless competition. It's not a place to "play office." If you think getting the best performance out of a man is going to come about as a result of you babying or nurturing him, you're not using your feminine power and leadership to scale the company. Men enjoy being acknowledged and recognized for action and results, especially when they've followed a command.

Commands don't need to be complicated. The shorter, the better. One time in the not too distant past, I received a text from my CEO in which he shared that we were creating a proposal to bid for a lengthy multimillion-dollar job with a prospect we'd been chasing for a long while. I wanted this client and naturally wanted to give my CEO all kinds of ideas on how to pursue it—all of which I had already taught him (in fact, he had surpassed my sales numbers long before that). After pausing to think about it for a moment, I decided to respond with only the simplest of commands, which I knew he would understand was related to our pricing strategy: "Be aggressive," I said, to which he replied, "Always."

DOUBLE STANDARDS

"You have a woman's tone of voice," the consultant said.

I stared at him, as my jaw dropped involuntarily.

My CEO, whom I'd worked with for over a decade, sat next to the consultant and they each looked at me as though waiting for a response. It was one of those moments where the little voice comes over a loudspeaker in your head and gives the sage advice of "If you can't say anything nice, don't say anything at all."

With a straight face, these two gentlemen were attempting to tell me why all of my suggestions were being taken as criticism by the CEO of my company. I had gotten involved again at an operations level that same year to break up some stagnation in our process improvement and company morale. I'd heard from multiple sources that the problem was a lack of alignment at the top, and I'd even had an executive assistant quit over it.

Remember early in this book when I said I would say some controversial things? I cannot leave out the fact that when certain messages come from a woman's voice, they are unfairly analyzed and sometimes taken the wrong way.

It was one thing to have an individual on the team react from their own personal childhood trauma, but to have a seasoned high-performance consultant sanction this "female voice" excuse for not being able to align with me absolutely bowled me over. What in the hell was I supposed to do? *I was experiencing discrimination in my own company.*

I searched my mind for how to respond to this situation. Granted, I had been well aware that early in my career, my tone would sometimes come across very differently to people than I intended it to. When I was in a state of reaction, I'd inadvertently make people think there was something very wrong or dire happening, whereas I was simply concerned. When our reactions are mixed with anxiety and worry, it doesn't work in an IFL's favor.

On the contrary, I have had several masculine business partners who were each far more adept at voicing concerns in a "normal" tone of voice. In turn, they get more matter-of-fact answers from others, and often they get more information as well. It's something I've had to work on.

I'm an emotional, intense person, but my team feels and knows I have their back. In my younger days, when I'd talk to people on the front lines about a glaring issue, I sometimes had to pause a day or two after I learned about it because to address it at the moment would bring too much intensity, causing a negative charge to ripple out to others. It comes with an entrepreneur's job to be surprised by miscalculations or misfortune from time to time. But there is a double standard in how people read reactions from women versus men, and it's not all in women's favor, to say the least.

That said, I'm thankful for the density (I mean it as a compliment in this context) of my masculine leaders. Particularly when I have taken huge risks or opened new business units in the past, I remember the tinge of terror that would come over me regarding something threatening about to happen. Yet when I'd share these concerns with the men on my executive team, my emotions would somehow dissipate without them even noticing what I was feeling. Masculine energy grounds me. If I had first spoken to some of the women on my team, chances are higher that my anxiety would have been contagious and multiplied. Occasionally (but rarely) have I been sucked into mild hysteria upon learning about issues from female staff members, which I later hear (usually from a man) have been blown out of proportion.

I really do think that men are more emotionally oblivious, so in stressful situations, it takes more to get them riled up. They just seem to handle a certain degree of pressure differently, at least in small to medium-sized businesses where corporate culture hasn't homogenized everyone. Some women *have* to talk about their feelings (I am one of them), while men don't (even though they probably should more often). Mind you, I'm talking about very subtle energetic patterns here, not overtly perceptible differences. Just know that when you talk about how you feel with intensity, there may not be a container big enough for you to "let it all out" and still be validated safely within your company. I recommend having a coach (or a therapist, if that suits you better) you can call for discussing things.

As a leader in business, you'll be better off if you're the one taking the fear *out* of every circumstance. Particularly in group meetings or when trouble is imminent or mistakes have been made, if you're known for bringing calm in situations, you create the space for the solution to emerge. Conversely, if you energetically lose your sh*t (even a little bit), people will avoid telling you things.

Here's a tip I can give you from personal experience: when you get upset, which is bound to happen, it's best only to point out the factual truth of *what happened* without emotional charge. Then add your observations regarding how to fix it, how to prevent it from happening again, and finally how to get everyone involved "put back together and whole" around what happened. Don't ever allow yourself to go on a tirade of suppositions. If you find yourself angry, it serves your team better just to state you're angry rather than slamming doors and so forth. That type of behavior causes invisible organizational trauma.

Remember, people are often listening more to our tone than to our words. It's not that they don't hear your words. Your words *are* being received by the neocortex, or the thinking brain. It's the tone that slips into the subconscious and is processed at a different level. If you're composed and in charge, your team will be more likely to follow you.

Since studies show that women are more likely to be chosen for leadership positions in times of crisis because they are seen as more emotionally fit for it, just focus on being your energetically balanced self when things get rough and you'll have the wind at your back. As the statistics show, your team will appreciate your perspective and the will of your feminine leadership.[50]

DEALING WITH SHADOWS

Carl Jung, the founder of analytical psychology, said the shadow is that part of the psyche that affects our behavior destructively. The human personality, he thought, is driven by unconscious and unknown desires, often dominated by this shadow—an inferior, unadapted, childish, and grandiose aspect of our unconscious life.[51] Because the shadows of a human carry so much inherent influence on a person's behavior, the best way to deal with shadows is to make them part of the game.

Before I talk about how to do that, my goals for this section are to help *set you free* from two things:

1. Thinking negatively of your shadow
2. Figuring out whose shadow is trying to thwart you so you can f*ck them up

If I accomplish these two goals, you'll liberate untold amounts of energy, which can be channeled back into setting and sustaining the optimum tone in your company. If you, as a leader, don't admit you're capable of operating from this dark place, you're more likely to be used by it. To be used by anything will cause you to make the mistake of focusing your attention (and the attention of your team) on distractions that should be inconsequential in the scheme of your big vision. This mistake is also called "majoring in the minors."

According to experts, not being aware of your less-than-altruistic motives means you're more likely to be exploited as a pawn for groups that are recruiting for a collective projection. I see this constantly in my CEO friends who sit from a one-up position and look down upon various types of people, such as political parties, age groups, religions, cultures, and other methods of dividing people. (And yes, I see it in myself.)

Only if you courageously understand what you're capable of as a human can you master being a benevolent leader. Jung believed that a person must actually embody their shadow, or their monster. "No tree, it is said, can grow to heaven unless its roots reach down to hell."[52] You do yourself (and everyone around you) a favor when you recognize that within you exists the capability of performing horrible acts. As a leader, that could include—but certainly isn't limited to—meanness, cronyism, corruption, or narcissistic decisions made under the intoxicating influence of power.

To realize this about yourself will make you more conscious of the judgments you put on others, which can be even more harmful coming from a CEO with power over people's future and daily lives. The leaders I know who are oblivious to their shadow are generally unaware of the power of their negative projections—which is nothing more than a defense mechanism you deploy when you take a feared weakness or unconscious negative element of yourself and redirect that self-loathing onto another person or group.

Most people frame the subject of shadows around the idea that we all have the potential for both good and evil. I see it as a bit more complex than being a matter of good and evil. (Otherwise, how could you have two sides of a fight believe they're doing good and the other side is doing evil? Who decides?)

Because we live on food instead of light (as plants do) and also because we have sex to procreate (as plants don't), we are fundamentally driven to "get something." It is this drive to "get something" that runs amok in the human, even though in our most awakened, Christlike state, we would rather love and be loved than compete, cause drama, and fight.

Once we realize that due to our endocrine system and the chemicals it releases we can be total scoundrels in an infinite number of ways, the challenge becomes how effectively we can (1) *discover* how our shadow operates and (2) *integrate* it into a plan of action to complement it with our higher-order thinking, while doing the same with our teams.

I've paid numerous coaches to reflect my shadow back to me, which throughout different times in my life has taken on different tones and forms. During one phase, my shadow took on the quality of domination (rooted in the need to avoid being dominated). In contrast, during another era in my career, I had a shadow of greed (which showed up as a scarcity mindset and preventing others from getting what they needed).

As I am writing this, my shadow has recently shown up as a habit of indicating to employees that I need them to have more integrity when I have caught myself telling bald-faced lies. I've also been invasively and incessantly "talking at" my young adult children about their futures as though they are still teenagers. Beneath that little gem of a habit, my shadow actually wants my kids to conform to my idea of success so they don't have to ask me for help later in life, and I can shake off the feeling that I might have messed them up by spoiling them. In other words, it's all about me.

Gross, right?

Are you getting the idea of how to uncover your shadow? If so, congratulations!

Do you see any new aspects of it after reading this? If so, even better!

"What the hell am I supposed to do with this information?" you may be asking.

The first step is to *accept the idea of a shadow*, which I assume you've already done after reading my synopsis of it and getting this far. The next step is to *start having fun with it.*

The absolute best CEOs I've known are those who account for and integrate their shadow into their awareness. In recognizing the shadow in themselves, they become skilled at *playfully* shining a light on the shadow of others. These leaders recognize that the shadow, or ego, can be framed or channeled in the context of business—as long as it's legal and ethical—and can provide juice or energy to the game.

Just like a player on the field or the court, everything that happens in your performance over time is a reflection of all the corners of your mind, not just the ones you talk about with other people. Therefore, and this is pretty advanced coaching, if you get honest with yourself, there are *no real surprises.* That we act surprised is just a joke that we play on ourselves. This brings us to my third step in dealing with shadows: *forgiving them, in yourself and others.*

Recognizing the particular qualities of your shadow, whether it's hubris, greed, hatefulness, jealousy, or the pathological need to be right, is very helpful when processing the constant feedback reflected by the universe. Playing with the collection of shadows created by you and everyone in your company, while simultaneously forgiving them, allows you to effectively deal with them as they arise and get in the way. Just be curious about the feedback the universe provides on your collective shadows and use it to reset the tone in your company again and again.

Unfortunately, no matter how effectively you deal with

shadows, they sometimes wreak havoc on human systems, putting us in situations we least prefer. In the next section, I address how to set the tone as an IFL when a situation has deteriorated into one of life or death for your company.

BEWARE THE FOG OF WAR

"Yes ma'am, I realize it's the week of Christmas."

Our global account executive spoke coolly to the company we'd hired in New York City to clean our corporate apartments. She was doing her part to save the company by persuading the cleaners to continue taking care of our rentals for thirty more days, even though we couldn't pay them. It was similar to the conversation our controller was having in the next room with the electric company, asking them not to shut off our services for not being able to pay our balance.

I'd been to three banks, business plan in hand, and was turned down three times for a line of credit. After seven years in business, an employee I had fired was now working for a competitor and was calling my company's clients while pretending to still be employed by us. In the process, she managed to poach a major account, just as another large project ended. Ironically, I also needed capital to fund a huge new one. It was the perfect storm.

"We understand that you really need to get paid, but we're having a slight issue with a large amount of money owed to us, and we'll need until next month to pay you. In the meantime, can you go ahead and clean the apartments so we don't have to find another company to work with?"

We had absolutely no way of knowing whether we'd be able to pay them the following month. Because I had taken on all of the personal debt (including the mortgage on a huge house) in my recent divorce, while the bank split my income level in half due to the partnership breakup, I wasn't an attractive borrower.

After a deafening silence, the cleaning company put us on hold, then called us back, then magically said yes, as did the furniture vendors, utility companies, and other cleaning companies across the country—all at the request of my team members, who humbly called and poured their authentic pleas for patience into the phone.

Finally, the fourth bank with whom I spoke loaned us $300,000, saving the company by allowing us to pay off vendors and fund the new project. (That was seventeen years ago, and my company is now that bank's largest customer.)

How we accomplished this whole miracle is something I think is essential to share, because you will be faced with at least a handful of these types of battles as an entrepreneur, and it's 100 percent up to you to set the tone in such a way that your team puts it all on the line to win. In the rare case you do get surprised by betrayal, a sudden economic hit, a lawsuit, or the loss of a key employee to your competitor, who happens to take your proprietary data, you need to be able to lead at your highest capacity from the eye of the storm.

The fog of war is what your team will experience when you (or your mission) are being attacked. Carl von Clausewitz, a Prussian general from the early nineteenth century said,

"War is the realm of uncertainty; three-quarters of the factors on which action is based are wrapped in a fog of greater or lesser uncertainty." When we were calling those vendors, it was based on a very difficult but clear-cut decision by our team. We chose to decree that "this will be our *finest hour*," which, of course, was borrowed from Winston Churchill.

In short, you must remember these simple instructions when you are placed in a situation that feels like life or death for your company: don't have an emotional response, and don't say anything that will make your opponent out to be a perpetrator while you appear as a victim. Remove any hints of it being personal. No matter how it looks, *it's not personal.*

Just sit before your team, take a few deep breaths, and relax. At this moment, because of what is happening and the fear they might be feeling, they will hear your every word, and they'll remember it for years to come, so let this be *your* finest hour. Tell your team that you *will* secure the ground that's been lost or threatened, but you will need their help.

Once you and your leadership team have absorbed the events of the day, and not before, respond with a strategy. Give the plan to your frontline employees in *single steps*, not all at once. They are not the visionaries, and they don't have to know the entire plan, because sometimes the fewer minds in the strategic process, the better.

During a battle like this, the weakest players must be placed in the background or removed until the company returns to wholeness. All liabilities must be mitigated. And remember, if everyone is in fight or flight, then no one is rational. So it's essential to keep your head as the leader, which means to keep your prefrontal cortex engaged. To maintain your state as an IFL, here are five ways to keep your prefrontal cortex activated during times of trouble:

1. Solve simple math problems or riddles, count something, name a group of things, or perform other tasks that reactivate the rational brain, especially if you get anxious.
2. Create a positive story of the future, which produces dopamine.
3. Make a list of one hundred things you are grateful for and feel your gratitude, which produces serotonin.
4. Move your body (e.g., sports, yoga, or dance).
5. Make positive physical contact (such as giving someone a big hug), which releases inhibitory peptides.

Once you've effectively taken back your ground during the fog of a battle, whether dramatic or subtle, it will be time to do some repairs.

CORPORATE SOUL RETRIEVAL: HEALING ORGANIZATIONAL TRAUMA

Not if but when your company experiences a significant adverse event, whether it's similar to the internal drama I just described or the impact of a sudden external phenomenon, like a crash in the economy, it requires you to do a reset on the tone of the company from one of shock, anxiety, or apathy (particularly with the loss of important clients or coworkers due to layoffs) to one of renewed hope and group coherence.

Therefore, any CEO can benefit from learning to perform

a healing process I like to call Corporate Soul Retrieval. I've performed this service on my own company several times and also on several of the companies I've consulted. If you don't feel comfortable doing things like this, I highly encourage you to find a consultant who might be able to help. You can find them under searches for consultants who help with corporate culture, change management, or employee engagement, and find one that feels compatible with your company's heart and soul.

"Soul retrieval" is a tool used by shamans to bring back lost pieces of the self. The basic premise of these healings is that when we've lived through trauma, a part of our life force has fragmented from us in order to survive the experience by escaping the full impact of the pain. This soul loss can cause a perpetual feeling of incompleteness and disconnection. In companies, it can lead to damaged culture, dissolved partnerships, or even slow death of the enterprise.

Corporate Soul Retrieval goes beyond healing the financial statements of a company and requires that you reflect upon the original spirit of the organization to reestablish everyone's connection to those roots. Although this complex process is difficult to express simply, I will describe the three main components that are common among all Corporate Soul Retrievals.

First, throughout the process, the executive team needs to embody the spirit of the company in any and all communications, mannerisms, and actions regarding the trauma. This is the equivalent of a paramedic not being upset when they arrive at the scene of an accident. Your executive team should understand that trauma happens, and when it does, the executives are the ones everyone is watching.

Second, leaders of the company must restate the highest objectives for how you'll continue to serve the customers and how what happened will help you achieve those long-term goals. This puts the team's analytical mind back to work and helps them get out of survival mode.

Finally, and this is the most important, it is the job of leadership to make each employee understand that what happened was traumatic, and it's normal to feel anything from fear to confusion to sadness to ambivalence. As the CEO, you will then follow up this validation with a statement that, as the one responsible, you will do everything in your power to prevent the trauma from happening again. (Then do it.)

These steps are not the end of the process but the beginning. To be a shaman in your own company, as you observe and identify missing elements, you'll need to bring back the lost fragments one by one. The retrieval of these lost aspects takes place during one-on-one conversations and team meetings, and within your internal dialogue. This can sometimes take months or even years to complete.

CHAPTER 6

DEAL WITH PRESSURE

The only gas pumps in town were occupied, with lines down a dusty road waiting behind each. The itty-bitty gas station was situated a few yards away from the only traffic light in a town of 697 people. Overworked men in hard hats, most of them at least a hundred miles from home, crowded the cash register to buy tacos, doughnuts, and coffee.

Out of nowhere, the extremely out-of-place sound of feminine enthusiasm grabbed all of their attention at once. "Hey, everybody! Come look at our furnished apartments!" emanated from a girl running toward them with flyers in her hands. This was her first week on the job, her first time selling, and her first time spending the night away from her husband. She was on the front lines of a battle I had started, another battle for the company's survival.

Tens of thousands of white trucks containing men in flame-retardant suits had descended upon one of the most remote areas of the country to work in one of the biggest oil booms in US history (the one I mentioned earlier). There wasn't enough housing, groceries, supplies, gas stations, or infrastructure to support them.

As such, I had just made a decision that put my company, and the jobs of everybody who worked there, at risk by renting an entire apartment complex to provide housing for the crews. Thankfully, the investment group who let me lease their brand-new, three-story property hadn't checked my balance sheet to determine whether I could afford the six-figure monthly rent.

It was late in the year, and we weren't even close to accomplishing our breakthrough sales goal for the year. What's more, I could see no possible way to achieve it. Truth be told, I had given up on that goal before our VP convinced me that, for her at least, *failure wasn't an option.*

We had recently lost a stream of government projects due to cuts in federal spending. Online booking platforms like Airbnb and others were killing off corporate housing companies left and right, making new business way more difficult to generate. And the global subprime mortgage meltdown had caused apartments to be in short supply, which made property owners unwilling to give us the terms we needed to sell our services at reasonable prices.

These macroeconomic factors were bigger than we could solve by hiring new salespeople. We needed to innovate, or the company would eventually die. Inspired by the vice president's kick-ass attitude and feeling guilty for letting her down with my apathy about these challenges, plus the goals we hadn't met, I made some calls to stir things up. One of those calls led me to an old friend who was building a new apartment complex in the middle of the oil patch. "I just need to lease these apartments up, and then I want to sell them," he said.

"I'll take them all," I said without hesitating.

Desperate times call for *desperate measures*.

Since there were no hotels to provide housing for workers, I'd decided to run the apartments like a hotel. I had seen corporate housing companies with this business model in Chicago, New York, and other places. Why couldn't an apartment hotel work in Carrizo Springs, Texas?

Once he figured out I was dead serious, he got his partners to agree. A few days later, my small business was on the hook for the vacant apartment complex. I had no money in the stock market because it always felt like a casino game to me. The only thing I'd ever really bet on was myself and my teammates. And this time, we had put it all on the line.

It was time to make the internal announcement and get buy-in, *and fast*.

"Okay everybody, here's the deal! I just leased 192 bedrooms in South Texas, and we're going to furnish them and run them like a hotel. I need you to get some heads in beds immediately, or we're going out of business."

Because we'd never been in the hotel business before, the team stared at me like I'd just flown in from Mars.

After borrowing $500,000 to furnish the apartments with

everything down to the can opener and putting up an internet tower and a sign that said, "Weekly Rentals," we were in business. Suddenly, the phone started ringing off the hook with developers from all over the United States who saw what we were doing and wanted us to do the same thing to their property. Within twelve months, we found ourselves under contract to run eleven properties as workforce hotels, including two dining facilities. We laughed, we cried, and we argued. There was a lot of excitement and confusion. *And there was definitely pressure.*

According to the Merriam-Webster dictionary, *pressure* as a noun is defined as:

1. The burden of physical or mental distress
2. The application of force to something by something else in direct contact with it

Regardless of how much grit, stamina, emotional intelligence, and physical health you embody, pressure is going to be a factor when you're starting or scaling a business. How we react to pressure as IFLs can be affected by the following three factors:

1. *Our physical state.* Our pressure response can be negatively impacted by things like poor sleep, lack of movement, situational stress, family issues, and addictions.
2. *Our ability to handle adrenaline,* which is partly given by one's current framework of neural networks or, more simply, one's thought patterns. This includes the ability to run situations through the prefrontal cortex (the thinking brain) and utilize alpha (relaxed) or theta (day-

dreaming) brainwaves when facing trauma instead of automatically going into fight-or-flight reaction.

3. *The energy of others.* We now know that the limbic system (a network of structures located beneath the cerebral cortex that is responsible for motivation and emotional behaviors) is an open system; thus, moods and tones are contagious.[53]

For as long as I can remember, I've been fascinated with these three elements regarding a team's capacity to handle the pressure of game time. As someone who grew up in an intense, pressure cooker of a household, I learned a variety of coping skills from a very young age. Because my feminine entrepreneur clients seem to have so much difficulty with pressure, I'm going to go a little more in depth with regard to the various ways I have learned to cope with it.

To begin, I have a "pressure quota," which is a minimum amount of pressure required to activate a certain level of focus for me. I prefer the positive, self-inflicted type of pressure—the same kind you'd experience performing or playing at the highest levels of a professional sport—but if I consistently experience the negative variety, I go over my quota more quickly and will retreat into my cave. What's the difference between positive and negative pressure, you ask?

It's a combination of things, but to me, much of whether pressure is desirable or destructive results from the story I tell myself about it. Remember the story about having to call vendors and tell them we won't be paying them over the holidays so they didn't revolt and get us fired from the project? Let's review some negative, neutral, and positive stories we could have told ourselves about that situation.

I invite you to think of a time in your life you could apply these as well:

NEGATIVE STORY	NEUTRAL STORY	POSITIVE STORY
How the heck did this happen?	It is what it is.	What an excellent problem to have!
What next?	Let's deal with it.	All hands on deck; let's do this!
Are you kidding me?	What's missing?	We've got this!
Ugh...why did this happen?	Who can solve this?	I chose to be here.
We've gotta figure out how to get out of this.	We'll get through it.	I am the one for this job.
I wish I could quit.	Stress is just the cost of doing business.	It's showtime!
How on earth did I get here?	You win some and you lose some. Hope we get this right!	This will be our finest hour.
I can't deal with this.	I wonder how we'll get out of this situation?	Bring it on!
Whose fault is this?		We were made for this!

This table illustrates my first coping skill as an IFL in the face of pressure, which is to deploy *asset thinking*, as we discussed in chapter 3. If you apply your asset (or winning) thinking to any pressure situation, along with taking some deep breaths designed to send signals to your nervous system that you're safe, you'll accomplish more than if you come at the issue from a place of fear.

I've even faked myself out by briefly imagining losing everything and starting all over again, focusing on relaxing into the worst-case scenario to let go of my terror. There are many ways that shifting your perspective will take you from *negative pressure* to *positive pressure* instantaneously. It is this shift that separates champions from runners-up.

The next coping skill I've reliably utilized to deal with negative, sustained pressure is *enlisting masculine support*, which I will talk about at length in chapter 7. I prefer enlisting masculine support because in my direct observation, as I said before, masculine figures don't seem to feel as much of the physical sensations that come with pressure and, on average, can handle this type of intensity *for longer periods*. That's why, on average, they tend to love contact sports, such as fighting, football, and so on.

The third, and arguably most important, coping tool I use against too much pressure is *self-care*. When I'm well taken care of, I can interact with others and make decisions in the most beneficial ways. To keep too much pressure from sapping my enthusiasm, creeping into my relationships, or affecting my health and well-being, I judiciously take self-care measures. Here are some of my favorite ideas for countering (or recovering from) pressure when I need a tune-up:

- Seek mentorship or coaching from someone who emulates what I seek
- Eat unprocessed foods, including superfoods/micronutrients
- Take supplements that support dopamine, serotonin, and relaxation
- Turn off the TV and stop following negative social media content
- Read uplifting articles or passages from classic spiritual texts
- Travel to a beautiful location
- Keep alcohol consumption low and water consumption high
- Take a warm, candlelit Epsom salt bath with music

- Avoid Debbie Downer and Grumpy Gus, or anyone who doesn't lift me up
- Take a moonlit walk or swim
- Get some extra sleep (like a solid ten hours on a weekend night)
- Meditate (use online apps or take classes if you don't know how)
- Receive touch (like massage, facials, pedicures, and of course, sex)

There are a multitude of ways to keep your energy clear by doing certain things and avoiding doing other things. When you deny yourself the things that do you harm, the body's natural, innate intelligence performs self-healing. Not to say that everyone is as sensitive as I am, but I know that if I'm consuming a lot of sugar, drinking alcohol, and eating inflammatory foods, I can't trust my thoughts as reliably. When I eat nutrient-dense foods and stay hydrated, my superpowers come back.

Beyond self-care routines for mind, spirit, and body, my entrepreneurial competencies also benefit from enlisting the help of assistants. At any given time over the years, this would include nannies, personal assistants, personal business managers, housekeepers, or household managers. At any given time, their title would depend on their skillset and what I felt like delegating during that period.

After working closely with me for a few months, sometimes these individuals get promoted to work in my company, or they transit to another career and move on. I've had some extremely amazing women and men as my assistants who have roughly served the same domestic support role that having a household partner would, and in that regard, each one made a unique contribution to my, and my kids', health and well-being.

Having a clean space is very grounding and gratifying, but at the end of the day, I don't want to decide whether to do a load of laundry or attend to a client. If the laundry wins out over the client, that could turn into a $50,000 load of laundry, and well, that's just not a good business decision. On the other hand, I'm too committed to having a clean house every day to let that load of laundry just sit there until I'm not busy. (Hence, hiring assistants.) Which brings us to the next section on how IFLs deal with pressure and where some of that pressure comes from.

WHAT TO DO WITH PERFECTIONISM

Just like it's impossible to sustain a whole house being perfectly clean and organized while at the same time occupying it, achieving perfection in a company is also impossible. You'll never, ever have all the plates spinning at the same time, and you never get to tie a neat little bow around it all. The thing about feminine beings is that, oftentimes, the pressure we feel is from a self-imposed condition called *being a perfectionist*.

There is, of course, an expectation placed on all leaders to convince our followers to *strive* for perfection. We're tasked with holding the vision of the perfect world and then asking people to translate it into reality by inspiring excellence. However, as an IFL you realize it's best to set up your people to win and not be demoralized by their many imperfections. To do this, it's best to understand the following about the nature of perfection:

1. PERFECTION IS ABOUT CONTEXT, NOT CONTENT.

For my perfectionist parents, effort was not enough. An impeccable outcome mattered more. They set the bar *extraordinarily high*, from how to perform chores to how I was supposed to speak to them. A psychologist might say they were compensating to prove they were "enough." Through learning and association, so too did their offspring. Thus, time and time again, my ability to strive for perfection while failing miserably has become second nature. The context set by my willingness to fail as the owner of the company, while being welcoming of the so-called mistakes of others, has created a robust framework for people to achieve amazing outcomes around me.

2. PURSUING *PERFECT MOMENTS* IS BETTER THAN SEEKING PERFECTION.

Imagine the bride and groom who meticulously design, schedule, and organize the food, drinks, flowers, music, and table settings of their wedding. But they forget to tell the cake maker there was a change in the time of the wedding months ago, so there's not a cake. *That's not perfect.*

Then the reception starts, the music plays, the ecstatic bride and groom walk in, people cheer, everyone raises a glass, and *ahhhh*...the anxiety is transformed into one of those absolutely perfect moments.

I recommend experiencing perfection by enjoying the *perfect moments* of daily life in your business. It can look like a celebration that makes your team belly laugh, the ringing of a bell when the client gives the team a high score, a beautiful acknowledgment of an employee, staging trivia contests at staff meetings, and so forth.

3. PERFECTION ISN'T ABOUT OUR SUBJECTIVE STANDARDS. IT'S AN IDEAL INSTALLED BY INFINITE INTELLIGENCE.

We love to observe flawlessness in various forms of human endeavor, whether the perfect execution of a Hail Mary pass in the last ten seconds of the football game or the goosebumps from hearing an opera singer perfectly hit a note. In business, expecting this type of flawlessness can be the enemy of productivity—the showstopper, the deadline destroyer, or the project killer. To get through the messy process of meeting a goal that your team took a stand for achieving, it's up to *you* to provide the connection to the higher purpose. Inspiring your team with the wisdom that they're building a cathedral, as opposed to just laying bricks, gives your organization that connection.

4. *SEEING PERFECTION* EXPANDS CONSCIOUSNESS, WHILE *PERFECTIONISM* CONTRACTS CONSCIOUSNESS.

Around perfectionists, nothing you ever do feels like it's good enough. In a company or a household, it's enough to make people walk around wound up tighter than eight-day clocks. The pursuit of perfection doesn't have to be that way. As an adult, I was fortunate to have two separate mentors who taught me to *see perfection*. This seems like a paradox, no? Seeing the perfection in everyone and everything is one way for you to see what's possible and have them see it too, especially during pressure situations.

GET HIT AND GET BACK UP

Mike Tyson once famously said, "Everybody has a plan until they get punched in the mouth." As a CEO, the hits you take could come in the form of betrayals, sabotage, lawsuits, losses of major clients, natural disasters, pandemics, recessions, or an ex-husband. These could all be reasons to throw in the towel, but successful business owners are the ones who can take energetic punches.

If you didn't think you were going to have to go through this at least a few times, you wouldn't own a business. Just remember, every time you take one on the chin, say to yourself, "Wow, that could have been so much worse." From the wisdom you accrue via playing the game, you learn not to be surprised. You also learn that when you expect things from someone else (i.e., results) and they expect things from you (i.e., bonuses, advancement), you're eventually going to be dealing with the egoic, shadow side of people.

In the past, I've had so-called loyal employees or contractors try to take me out (directly or indirectly) with extortion, fraud, theft, breaking noncompete clauses, dereliction of duties, and miscellaneous sordid activities. The only way I've survived multiple hits like these is to see my business as a spiritual path and take 100 percent responsibility, whether it was caused by my having a cloudy assessment of a person or situation or outright mismanagement. I know this goes against many people's grain, but I prefer it to be that way because it keeps me in an empowered place.

Some hits are from people who wouldn't throw a punch but who use their words to cut like knives. In my experience, this has usually come from other women who are competing for positions in an invisible, imaginary social-status hierarchy. They not only wholeheartedly believe in this as a reality, but they invest their time and energy in creating it. Unfortunately, some of those women don't realize their function is leadership, and as a result, they find themselves unconsciously creating a low-level game to play.

It makes one wonder, what is it that they're not getting at home or from their life? Where are they not complete? What is it that makes them feel the need to gossip and complain so much? In all fairness, I'd probably be playing similar games as well if I didn't have the game of business. I'd constantly be promoting myself on Facebook, gossiping about people, and positioning myself for glory in my small village.

In psychology, the term *dissociation* refers to a mental process where a person disconnects from their thoughts, feelings, memories, or sense of identity. While in psychology it generally has a negative connotation, in business it can be quite practical, especially when people and problems are coming fast and hot from all different directions. To bring home the sports metaphor, if you choose to be a participant in a game, and you get injured while playing, you don't quit the game altogether. You allow some time to rest and recover. Then you get your ass back on the field.

LOVING IT

In college, I believed that any and all observable differences between men's and women's behavior were caused by social programming. Today, based on more than twenty-five years of coaching thousands of colleagues and employees, my beliefs regarding male and female behavior have changed. I still don't know if these gender distinctions are from nature or nurture, but there are some general observable trends when it comes to the subject of pressure.

Although I have rare IFL friends and clients who thrive on complexity, mitigating risk, overcoming adversity, and proving haters wrong, most of the people I've worked with who describe themselves as entrepreneurs (but are actually solopreneurs, in reality) would rather not deal with the pressure of great challenge. They want comfort, reassurance, and to be soothed. This section is for them.

Having challenges doesn't need to be scary. To have a challenge does *not* require you to feel like something's wrong. To be challenged is simply admitting, *I have some uncertainty or doubt concerning my ability to perform or execute upon a particular issue or task.* Then, if you can take away that doubt, what you are left with is resolve, and through the declaration of your resolve and feeling it in your body, you disempower doubt.

No matter the processes, systems, and people you put in place, your best intentions will be thwarted. When things get rough—if you lose your cool in a big way when your best-laid plan falls apart, your reaction can (and likely will) be felt throughout your entire organization. If you wind up doing this frequently—and it, in turn, becomes your communication style—your team may wind up holding back, freezing up, or second-guessing themselves.

As a result of this break in the flow of energy, which all starts with you—instead of your team using the creative, rational parts of their brains, they will act from the amygdala, which is the part of your brain that governs your senses, muscles, and hormones concerning the sight or sound of threats. What this ultimately looks like is your team showing up as less competent, which is going to *really* piss you off, and once again, you're back to the beginning of a negative circle.

Don't be that leader.

The antidote to challenges is to talk to your team about your challenges and turn solving them into a game. For a person who thrives on productivity and efficiency, bad moods cost money. For highly productive people, they cost even more. As an example, if you have a bad mood for two to three days, there is no way to calculate all the resistance, pressure, domination, avoidance, withheld communication, physical stress, and other damage that has been done.

The net effect can hurt your cash flow for days, weeks, or even months. An average millionaire who has a bad mood might inadvertently cause hundreds of thousands of dollars in indirect costs or lost opportunities. What are you willing to allow your moods to cost you? Being a moody martyr is definitely not worth the short-term payoff.

MAKE PEOPLE BRILLIANT

When the pressure is on you in business, the quickest way to relieve that pressure is to connect to your team members and empower them to assist you. In order to do that, you'd better believe they actually *can* help you, or your doubt will contaminate their results. Disbelieving that at least a couple of your teammates can perform at the same level as (or better than) you is also one of the surest ways to go from inspired to uninspired. If you have a hard time putting faith in your team to perform under pressure, you either (1) have the wrong team, (2) haven't trained them, or (3) haven't put them in situations where they can prove themselves.

Or maybe you're a control freak.

One of the observable laws of business that gets broken a lot is to *expect your team to be brilliant*. As I've alluded to, some of us have a regrettable tendency to make ourselves overly important to an organization by making ourselves indispensable, and this can and will slow down our own growth and the growth of the company.

Being your hypercompetent, brilliant self while treating teammates as less than brilliant is a *huge* leadership mistake. Instead, you should do whatever it takes to shine a light on your team's abilities *in advance* of their own belief in themselves.

Not just to make them look brilliant but to give them the mindset and autonomy to do their own thing. This includes giving them more responsibility than they think they're ready to handle, providing them with proper training, and coaching them on how to handle their new role and responsibility.

In companies, anyone who is incapable of letting go and letting her team perform not only is trapping herself in dealing with pressure more often than she should, but she's stunting her teammates—*which gets noticed by company leadership and makes them resistant to promoting her.* Consequently, people who get promoted are the ones who force employees under them to step up by putting them in situations where it's required.

In my experience, it's men who are better at doing so. In many of the companies I've worked with, the average masculine leader does not get lost in the weeds. Instead, by becoming an effective delegator, he lets his team handle the details, sometimes to a fault. He then gets promoted because management says, "Look what he has done with his teams."

In the long run, being indispensable is how otherwise competent people screw up businesses beyond all recognition. The "I'm the Lone Ranger, and no one else can do it like I can" syndrome is why, when a firm gets acquired, one of the first things to happen is that all the so-called sacred cows get slaughtered. Many of those sacred cows are the people who thought the organization couldn't live without them, and that's precisely why they are taken out.

CHAPTER 7

ENLIST MASCULINE SUPPORT

While women were integral parts of agrarian and mercantile entrepreneurship before the industrial revolution,[54] the hierarchical workflows of large and industrial corporations (and governments) were designed from a masculine perspective. Until we come to realize this, we won't be able to see, reveal, and utilize women's greatest leadership strengths at the highest levels. As men come to realize the need for more balance within themselves, they will better appreciate collaboration and an "everybody wins" attitude. But until then, I'm a strong advocate for (1) starting your own company and (2) making your own organization balanced through the presence of both masculine and feminine energy.

Remember, the research shows there is a glass ceiling/cliff and, as of this writing, only 7.6 percent of CEOs in the Fortune 500 are females. And remember that *no one has been able to solve this glass ceiling/cliff with diversity programs, inclusivity metrics, and motivational efforts.*

Hundreds of thousands of women are quitting, are opting

out, or aren't showing up for promotions to top leadership roles because we refuse to be politically incorrect and address what is really causing the problem. We haven't changed the nature of work, in general, to bring a balance of feminine ways of doing things. Therefore, we continue to condition women to believe we need to show up as masculine in corporate cultures that reward extreme personal sacrifice and in which men are willing (albeit many of them unhappily) to make those sacrifices.

When we show up as *feminine* females, we are disregarded in the hierarchy as being weak or invisible. In my view, this is why the "broken rung" phenomenon is happening. Feminine females *don't even get promoted to frontline management.*

I think it totally sucks that feminine traits are sometimes still mistakenly seen as weakness. But the fact remains that people at the highest levels of business have to very quickly surmise whom they can count on when a fortune is at risk.

I've engaged in business transactions, projects, and initiatives with masculine military leaders, corporate managers, real estate developers, financiers, and countless private-sector CEOs throughout the United States, in Europe, and in Central and South America. I've attended meetings, collaborated, and built friendships with thousands of masculine business leaders.

Occasionally, there is another female or two in the forefront of these discussions, but it is rare. I guess you could say I've operated in almost exclusively male-dominated environments. I have my own body of evidence for offering the following tips and have come to these observations honestly. What I've experienced has informed my passion for bringing about a balance of masculine and feminine energies on earth, not the disappearance or homogenization of them. So, without further ado, let's get into why enlisting masculine support plays a part in that balance and how it can support you in staying at the top as a feminine entrepreneur.

It's been my observation that in companies (large and small) where men are in power, they will consciously or subconsciously try to diminish (or worse, sabotage) the power of a competitive female leader who is in her masculine energy. It used to piss me off like nothing else until I learned it wasn't personal. One of the aspects that made me so angry about this behavior was that, as powerful and gritty as I am, it felt like an unfair fight. It felt like the cards were stacked against me.

It doesn't take a rocket scientist at a whiteboard to explain that if you place a male and female in a boxing ring, the majority of the time, the male is going to win. Some people may say this analogy is misguided, but I disagree because, as I've mentioned, taking hits is part of a business leader's job.

But taking more hits than necessary is just stupid. Men built hierarchical companies around their systems, their proclivities, and their hormones. They don't just compete with business competitors; they are happy to compete with coworkers inside of an organization. It's in their biological nature, not just in their cultural programming, particularly if they are (as many of them are) themselves out of balance and not at all in touch with their own feminine energy.

Therefore, it's wise to think twice before showing up every day as a masculine figure. If you do, please understand that depending on the environment, you're putting yourself in a situation in which you might be taken out. It might be via comments behind your back or redirected projects that should have been yours, but make no mistake—it *will* be passive-aggressive—because most men won't be aggressive toward a woman.

When I stay in my masculine side for extended periods, not only do I feel the energetic hits; I also get disregarded and competed against time and time again, which feels like discrimination. But they also do that to each other. The only way I've won, while keeping my inspiration levels high, is to bring out my feminine self and collaborate with them in a way that looks slightly different than how they work with each other.

On the one hand, when you consciously or subconsciously try to be a better man than a man, you're going to fall short a large percentage of the time. While the tendency is to think that conforming will help you get to the next level, the more you do, the more gradually you begin to lose touch with your natural state.

On the other hand, by staying in your embodied feminine energy, you might feel like you are invisible. You may even get passed over, left out, patronized, or appeased—*unless* you collaborate and create synergies with influential male leaders by being yourself and letting them be who they are.

This is how you avoid the glass cliff: start your own f*cking company and bring in masculine figures to take your hits *when you don't feel like it, just like you hire someone to change your tire if you don't feel like it.*

This is the only solution I've found to the glass ceiling/cliff that doesn't involve you growing a pair or changing who you are to succeed. While you can't change an entire corporate culture yourself, when you start your own company, you can create your own rules—rules that are simpatico with the way you like to lead.

Now, let's get back to enlisting masculine support. I had an all-female staff for a few years, but I have now found that when we have a substantial amount of masculine energy on our leadership team, our female VP and I have more fun and stay more relaxed while still getting done what we want to be done—and it's usually done (more or less) how we want it. Mind you, we spent many years *not* intentionally enlisting masculine energy, and we fulfilled our duties just fine, but the cost put my body under immense physical and emotional pressure. That is why I make no apologies for doing it this way, and I hope it provides you some insight as to how to grow your company without wanting to quit when it gets extremely stressful.

I know several masculine CEOs whose revenues range from the hundreds of millions to multiples of billions. These men have deep respect and understanding for placing women in the executive suite. The irony is, when we're talking about their businesses, what they say to me most frequently is, "I wish there were more women in leadership."

I ask them, "What would happen if more companies (and

governments) opened up a dialogue to realize the higher value of *feminine* leadership instead of *female* leadership?"

Generally, they fall silent, either because they're uncomfortable talking about gender differences or because they don't think feminine leaders would be a good idea (LOL).

Besides these lovers of women and what they bring to the table, unfortunately, some men would sooner cut off a testicle than be an ally for female representation. At some point along the journey of your career, you'll recognize this tiny number of men who share a common trait: they are broken in their relationship with women and "the feminine." I'm no therapist, but it seems like at least some of them are reacting to the separation-based feminist culture and/or gender-identity politics. In contrast, others somehow learned to devalue feminine traits and are mistaking your kindness for weakness.

Luckily, this is only a minority of men. You'll save yourself a lot of agitation by not trying to change these individuals. Instead, engage directly with the ones who aren't broken and who recognize and feel your powerful contribution... then dial up your efforts to match theirs. They will appreciate and respect you for it.

INTERDEPENDENCE, NOT DEPENDENCE

I was raised to be independent—to not ever rely on a man for support. It's an art I have mastered, yet what's been most rewarding has been the process of learning to be *interdependent*.

When I was speaking in front of women's groups and leading workshops, I wasn't initially aware of the alienation some professional women were feeling toward men. That is until I heard a woman in one of my seminars say, "I'm so glad I attended your workshop because I didn't realize until now that I hated men."

To which I replied, "*Wow*, thank you!" But I was thinking, "OMG. Seriously?"

Then, I realized two things: (1) how glad I was that she attended my workshop and (2) how much more money she would earn through the rest of her career as a result of no longer resenting men. This surprising aspect of my training was actually the seed that began me thinking along the lines of "Perhaps, I should do more of this working-with-female-entrepreneurs thing."

Because it's trendy at the moment to be a "stick-it-to-the-man" ultrafeminist, I know a few women who would rather be broke than partner on a business project with a man who doesn't share her values and who has a traditional mindset when it comes to gender roles. In the business world, these women are limiting their income and status while ensuring undue hard work and sacrifice. Ironically, many of these women aren't being feminine at all, which is pretty much the point of having more female leaders.

Just like your own shadow, the shadow aspects of a masculine figure come from his ego, which gets even more inflamed when confronted with an opposing ego. It's useless to fight against them. *So what the hell do we do?*

The answer is to *love them*—love them for who they are,

what they are, and what they bring to the table. There's no place for trash-talking in an Inspired Feminine Leader's vocabulary. Instead, she works *with* potent masculine powers rather than *against* them, *leveraging* their strength so as to do her heavy lifting. And, ladies, there is a lot of heavy lifting in business. If you want to do it all yourself, well, that's great, but you don't have to.

THE BOYS' CLUB

I've read a few articles and even a book or two that offer women guidance as to how to make their way into the alleged "boys' club." I know the methods well, and I am also familiar with the limitations and drawbacks of deploying them.

In order to be accepted into this boys' club, you must first realize it's not a club. *It's hundreds of millions of clubs.* Second, you need to realize they're not exclusive clubs (with some exceptions, of course). For the most part, they're simply tight, close-knit groups of people that happen to be composed of men, and so, as a result, they have distinctly masculine traits and cultures. As a woman, I've been discriminated against when trying to join some of these cliques simply because I'm a woman; I've been denied from entering others for reasons that have nothing to do with gender; and to others, I've been welcomed with open arms.

The thing is, none of them were actual just-for-men clubs. They were *networks of trust and admiration,* with the intent of mutually assured success. Just as women know how to exclude, so too do men. It's not personal. How I got into the ones I got into was by *not* trying to be like them.

Instead, I was being myself and letting them be themselves; all the while, we helped each other attain what we wanted.

I wish it weren't true, but on some profound level, under the surface of comradery and joviality, I have discovered that the pivotal business conversations men conduct with each other are tests as to whether or not they can bet their life on the deal, the team, or the partner. As you find yourself in these conversations, there are a few things that will have you pass this test and some that will have you fail it. If you resent the fact that this test exists, I recommend relaxing around the truth that our species would not have survived without men acting in such a manner. So instead of looking at it as a test, have fun, relax, and weave your own style into the situation or environment. And if they don't let you in? To hell with them. It's their loss.

When you're dealing with men, if everybody knows where they stand, and there's a sense of nonjudgment in a group (aka a team), their intense joking and well-placed insults can be quite fun and even hilarious. If you can handle this and laugh with the best of them, you'll be invited deeper into the circle of trust. If you want to be an uncompromisingly powerful CEO, you should probably immediately get over being easily offended.

There is one important caveat to this, and I want you to hear this from me rather than learning it the hard way: when you try throwing jabs with the boys, please know that for a variety of reasons, they don't enjoy zingers coming from a woman so much. It took me a loooong time to learn that men's egos are more apt to be bruised by a female than a male, and they also don't feel it's appropriate to insult you, so it's not a fair situation for them.

While, obviously, you know the line where fun ends and harassment begins, when you allow men to be masculine and you enlist their support in *your* game, you're going to experience them (at least healthy, nonpredatory males) being more open, generous, and protective, and you'll also enjoy a happy, healthy bank account due to the access this provides.

STRAIGHT LINES VERSUS CIRCLES

In my experience, this distinction between masculine versus feminine communication is a big deal. From my perspective, it seems feminine managers and leaders tend to naturally speak in concentric circles, with each sentence spoken getting increasingly closer to the heart of a topic. It follows that, as a CEO, my vital conversations with female managers have been most effective through indirect persuasion and building their confidence in my plan rather than being direct all the time. For instance, when I want to make a change that will impact them, I might first assure them that I can see everything that's working well and that these areas need to be protected. Then, I might set a context for what I think is possible if we adjust, including how it will make things easier on them in the long run.

As the stakes rise, this empowerment style seems to help them stay aligned. As we disseminate information to our team regarding the plan we're executing, my feminine leaders tend to ensure I have insight into all possible scenarios. (In other words, they are proactive about telling me everything that can and will go wrong.)

With masculine leaders, however, I've found I must be more direct in stating the intention early on. This is for two reasons: (1) the masculine leaders I've worked with hate what they call "beating around the bush," and (2) an instruction to them that isn't clear and well defined is perceived as a mere suggestion. As an example, imagine programming a computer. What happens if you miss one command? The program doesn't work. Likewise, the opposite is also true— if you add *too much* nonapplicable information, it also won't work. Women are the opposite. We function no matter how much information is coming at us or if a small piece is missing. We're able to focus on it all in a diffused manner.

I have employed a cadre of extremely feminine male assistants over the years, several of whom have told me they are more in touch with their feminine side than their masculine side. Yet, when I would give them instructions, I'd have to be black and white. With actual female assistants, I can give them the general idea of what I'm looking for, and it gets done.

LEADING MASCULINE LEADERS

In the interest of you being an efficient IFL, here are several tips on leading male leaders. Hopefully, my hard-won experience will help you, despite the potential controversy it may stir. While some of these may seem obvious, I can tell you from experience they are tried and true.

Tip #1: Instead of pretending everyone is the same, notice what tasks, negotiations, or conversations would be better suited for a masculine figure instead of a feminine figure, and vice versa. Although it would be considered heinously inappropriate in a large corporation, it's fun to experiment and watch how differently things go when you put a couple of guys on a challenge and then a couple of women. It is a total hoot to see how differently they go about it, while each is effective (most of the time).

Later in my career, I started experimenting with having men on our team spark conversations that would benefit us by being represented by a masculine character. They'll gladly make a phone call that none of our feminine leaders want to make. Believe me, I would have never, ever thought of doing this until I consciously decided to maintain my feminine energy. Then I mentioned it to one of our female managers, saying, "I want to let a man handle this," to which she replied, "Thank you."

When we tripled our revenues and our employee count in six months, I had an executive team of four women. We handled the ensuing chaos as professionals, but that's not to say it was relaxing or fun. Two of the women turned on the other two, and then they turned on me. I didn't catch it in time, and as a result, I ended up losing three of the four women executives. We eventually tracked the whole issue to an act of sabotage by one of the women whom we had recently hired. She dismantled the next company she worked for as well, leaving a trail of destruction and lawsuits in her wake. It's good to have feminine radar from good women who have integrity. But you can't trust them all.

Immediately after the shake-up, I decided to promote two of the men on my team—men who had already made it clear they were capable of handling pressure with ease instead of passing it around to each other. In times of great stress,

I've also had masculine team members drive me on long-distance road trips for meetings in the oil field. Their lack of idle chitchat and hyperfocus on driving (instead of being self-conscious) allowed me to stay relaxed, focused, and in my genius zone.

When "game time" came, and we were all sitting around a negotiating table, this kind of basic support helped immensely to ensure the desired outcomes. During meetings of great consequence, I've also covertly arranged them next to me at the table, asking them for a bottom-line, black-and-white perspective on problems so I could stay in a more feminine, holistic, fluid perspective—including observing the energies around the room.

Tip #2: Masculine leaders respect IFLs who are masterful at controlling their emotions, especially when provoked. (I could write a book on the double standards of the masculine and feminine dynamic at work, but it wouldn't get us anywhere. Let's focus on working with them because working against them hasn't yielded the results we seek.) *Onward...*

Have you ever seen the movie *Zero Dark Thirty*? Based on the true story of how Osama bin Laden was taken out, the movie portrays a female CIA agent who faces off with the Navy SEAL team leader assigned to infiltrate bin Laden's Pakistani compound under cover of night. Although the mission had been approved, she faced multiple levels of opposition that would have made most bureaucrats quit. During a heated exchange, the SEAL leader was looking for any molecule of hesitation, fear, or worry. Still, she stood her ground, returning his glance with confidence that conveyed she was willing to bet her career (and their lives) on her inner knowing.

This exchange, along with her standing up for her convictions in the face of no support from the director of her agency, resulted in putting approximately twenty-four of the United States' finest Navy SEALs, along with the institution's reputation, on the line. We all know what happened with that one.

Tip #3: Limit opinions, hunches, or pure intuitions you deliver that don't have any accompanying data-driven information or specific examples. Like everyone, masculine leaders typically have a good reason for why or how they are doing certain things. Therefore, they appreciate you being curious about what that reason is before insinuating something needs to change. Also, imagine that what you say will be taken very literally and that it will be remembered for a very long time. Men don't give you the benefit of changing your mind about things as easily as your female leaders will. They take what you say more definitively, so be careful.

One other thing: women see everything that could go wrong as being important to consider, so sometimes we lose people's faith. Ironically (and sadly), our radar abilities are a double-edged sword. We have a vivid picture of various outcomes, and the challenge is not to let our steady stream of concerns take our team off its focus, or it will become a self-fulfilling prophecy.

Tip #4: A surefire way to always connect with a masculine leader—in *any* environment—is acknowledgment

and appreciation for their contribution. This method applies in connecting with anyone, but I am mentioning it specifically as a tip for interacting with masculine leaders, because in my experience, they actually get very little acknowledgment from each other, as women do. When you acknowledge and appreciate your masculine leaders, letting them know that something they're doing for you and/or the organization is greatly appreciated will create openness to collaborating with you. Even if you have to give constructive feedback, beginning and ending with acknowledgment is vital—not only for the results they're creating in the organization but also for how brilliantly they accomplished it.

Tip #5: Let them know you also have an ass-kicking side and that you're not afraid to use it. Ideally, if all is going well, it's not necessary to step into your masculine energy, but when I have to put my foot down or protect myself, I drop it like it's hot. According to cognitive-behavioral scientists, our masculine protector side is called our *anima*. Over two decades, the several times I've unleashed my anima, I let my masculine side be as brutal as the situation required, for as long as it dictated. But I know that as I grow the business, if I don't keep my feminine side alive, my brutal masculine side will become my state of being. And that, as we know by now, is not how IFLs operate.

CHAPTER 8

TEN LOSING STRATEGIES

To have the freedom afforded by being your own boss, it's beneficial to sidestep certain pitfalls, or you'll end up wasting time and losing revenue. Some of these pitfalls I've turned into a list of losing strategies—each of which I've seen entrepreneurs inadvertently deploy while pushing business away. Some of these "ways of being" destroy credibility, and others create an invisible disease inside your company, which kills it over time.

Because you're an entrepreneur, you're not interested in playing unproductive games. You're too busy looking for ways to *be better than you used to be* and *do better than you used to do*. You're classy, not trashy.

If any of the following losing strategies seems to hit too close to home, I recommend that you (1) make a new choice and (2) take bold, corrective action—even if it causes your friends and family to think your standards have become a little too high.

Without any further delay, here are the top ten losing strategies I've seen women, including feminine entrepreneurs, play in the world of business:

LOSING STRATEGY #1: BEING ANTIBUSINESS

Some people despise the "business side" of actually doing business. I know this may seem ridiculous to some, but you'd be surprised how many wannabe feminine entrepreneurs I've seen have a problem with wealth, capitalism, and so on. While you are most likely excited about providing a service and working with people to solve problems while getting paid well for it, others subconsciously despise it. I have also seen some so-called entrepreneurs have a holier-than-thou, "this constant focus on earning is so beneath me" air about them.

Don't start a business if you hate the wealthy or people who are always focused on being productive.

LOSING STRATEGY #2: NOT HAVING THE BEST COACHES

Hiring a coach is a worthy investment, not just in yourself but in your business. It can also be a valuable investment for certain leaders on your team.

Coaches reflect your own greatness back to you, but they expect you to bring that greatness forth. A coach might reflect to you whether you're playing too small or might point out when an idea does or does not bring you to life. Are you tolerating or avoiding a problem? Are you giving your team the right tools to set them up for the win?

A great coach asks the right questions and can help take

you out of the heat of the moment. Their currency is fierce, unrelenting *love* for you and your vision, and when you falter, if you feel as if you can no longer stand in that vision, like a defensive line, they will hold the ground for you. So if you're in the game in between plays, you need to have someone on the sidelines whom you can look to for observations and guidance.

When you think of coaching, remember, it does not have to be one-on-one. You can also find executive education groups, like Vistage Worldwide or EO (Entrepreneurs' Organization). Just do your research to find the one that's right for you.

LOSING STRATEGY #3: GOSSIP AND COMPLAINING

At any level of an organization—but particularly at the top—the communication patterns of gossiping, complaining, and/or blaming are not compatible with success. In my companies, I have always viewed the rise of gossiping, blaming, and/or complaining as a potential symptom of a glitch in our organization's operating system.

The IFL realizes perfectly well that when someone gossips, complains, or blames, they're seeking agreement or validation on a point of view. This validation is part of their survival strategy, since the number one subconscious fear wired into humans is *fear of abandonment*. This allows you to delve into the *root cause* of a low-vibe communication instead of being sucked into taking a hard position on something.

When gossip goes unchecked in the company culture, it

creates damaging, *unproductive agreements* about people, projects, and circumstances. When the gossip comes from you, an IFL, it's even more damaging. One strategy is to do what coaches call *vote the victory* of the person who is gossiping or blaming, as well as the person who is being discussed. *Voting everyone's victory* changes how you respond, what you're willing to say, and whether you add fuel to the gossip or remove its oxygen source. This way, no matter how juicy the private chatter is, you'll stop the spread of negativity in its tracks while elevating the vibe for all parties involved by getting to a solution.

The first cousin of gossiping is complaining. Besides having been found to make people less smart, the habit of complaining presents a coaching opportunity for an IFL. When someone complains, there is a *commitment* behind it. Your mission—should you choose to accept it—is to find their underlying commitment without enrolling in the complaint. Look past the tone and hear the message *behind* the message—especially if the person in front of you isn't clear on the *root cause* of their issue. Figuring out what positive outcome the person is trying to get accomplished (despite their negative communication pattern) can help them break the pattern.

You can also do this when you hear yourself complaining. If a complaint comes out of your mouth, what are you committed to that isn't being honored, and what can you do about it?

LOSING STRATEGY #4: GENDER TRIBALISM AND THE MALTREATMENT OF MEN

To those who automatically assume this section does not

apply to them, or maybe don't believe this behavior exists, you might want to lean into the idea that the patriarchy suppresses the feminine perspective and feminine energy within *both* genders, leading men into a state of shame, where we then pile on more guilt.

The trending encouragement of female entrepreneurs to stick together, have each other's back, and not connect with men emphasizes, breeds, and reinforces separation.

Maybe it's because I have a son whom I'd take a bullet for, or maybe because I've been guilty of it myself (being trained by imbalanced female figures from childhood to make men wrong for certain things, such as being themselves), but I've witnessed a special type of meanness reserved for men... and it wrenches my gut.

When a man is a rough-cut stone, we can help polish him. It's better to bring him into a balanced state of being through compassionate, inquisitive, accepting engagement. This is a state of being that allows you to share, express, and accentuate your feminine perspective—so as to allow for creativity (and sometimes healing) to arise.

I bring this topic up because, in workshops and seminars that I've led, I repeatedly get asked about this. The maltreatment of men is really a thing, and it's an equally impactful issue in the realm of gender equality as the equality and safety of women. (Do you take care of your daughters before your sons? No. You take care of all of them.)

It takes a relatively toxic person to think that masculinity in itself is toxic. Criminal behavior, misogyny, racism, and physical, mental, and emotional abuse—these are toxic behaviors. But since the dawn of our ancestors organizing into tribes and communities, violence has had its place (protection), power has had its role (leadership), and dominance (survival) has had its purpose.

I love masculinity, even if some men are prone to their own types of aberrations. In an ideal world, aberrations of such types would not be on the receiving end of shaming judgments. These men would have a chance to tell their own stories or early trauma, and the planet's rigid patriarchy would crumble with a love earthquake.

Since these types of behaviors do not occur in nature, it means they are learned, which means, as with most people, there was some sort of wound along their journey. Rumi said, "The wound is the place where the Light enters you." When something bad happens, and you can't process it emotionally, the likelihood of being a perpetrator is huge.

If that imbalance of masculinity was met with the exact corresponding strength of femininity, the malignant behaviors that grew out of those wounds would *not* be met with judgment and shame, but rather with *healing, reform,* and *acceptance.* This is the power of the feminine energy, to provide healing through the restoration of balance—as within, as without.

Rather than ask men to tone down their masculinity, I think a reprogramming has to occur, and it starts with our children. Programming, deprogramming, and reprogramming—these are loaded terms in this day and age. All I mean is that it needs to be safe for men to express their feelings, emotions, or empathy.

Not just for men—but for any human—to not be able to express oneself is to allow a logjam to occur in the river of your being. It starts innocently enough with twigs connecting with other twigs. Those configurations snag on the river's edge and connect with more configurations of broken branches and debris, and before you know it, there is no more flow occurring. From one side of the dam, everything looks fine, but from the other, there is a mounting pressure that is just waiting to explode.

And that's not a bad thing. In combination with the way boys are raised, the different perspectives you'll find men generally bring comes down to the chemicals our bodies create. To magnify that idea from chemistry to gender and sociology, it's not healthy (whether on the micro or macro) for us to dislike or resent the way men think, act, or express themselves from their masculine perspective. *Nothing* we say or do is going to change them, and to try to repress that masculine expression—well, mark my words—we will suffer the consequences in ways that haven't been calculated.

If you're the owner of a company, and you not only value but desire the insights, observations, and/or financial forecasts of a man's perspective, then—to once again be colorful— you're going to have to strap on a set. You have to be open to his honesty, which sometimes comes with a certain level of bluntness. Chances are likely he's not even aware he's delivering that unfiltered perspective.

When I bring my CEO an idea that within me is brimming, overflowing, and exploding with excitement—and in the course of a five- to ten-minute dialogue, he dismembers it—you might think I'd feel upset and invalidated, right?

Nope. This level of feedback is precisely the reason why I want that person as a sounding board and on my team.

First, I appreciate his perspective, and second, he's able to separate and untangle complex patterns I wasn't able to see. Even though, over time, I've developed additional senses for particular things (which, as a CEO, you will discover through the experiential process of being challenged in new ways), I'd rather win the game than score all the points.

It's like this, ladies: you can't have the benefit of a male perspective and, at the same time, take away his control or agency. In other words, you can't expect to have a strong man under your tutelage if he isn't allowed to express himself as a man.

I believe this meanness, this shaming of men from women, is rooted in resentment. Men should *not* try to behave more like women. That's a misunderstanding. Men should be men, within whom exist a vast spectrum of behaviors and energies—all of which complement and counterbalance our vast spectrum of behaviors and energies.

LOSING STRATEGY #5: FEEDING DOUBT

The virus of doubt can invade the best ideas, people, and projects. If one were to place it in a petri dish, you'd find it grows best in conditions of organizational or personal incoherence and lack of alignment. Don't let the fact that this is number five on this list fool you—doubt is a project killer for entrepreneurs.

Sadly, I see women doubt themselves first and others

second...while with men, it's the other way around. We've been programmed to buy the negative script in our heads for some reason. Of course, this doesn't apply to all women all the time, especially IFLs. But before we get into that, first, we need to distinguish doubt from fear.

Fear can be a useful tool. Its intelligent design is twofold: (1) it keeps us out of danger, and (2) it forces us to overcome our edges, which is where real growth occurs. Let's break that down one step further—while a little bit of fear is healthy, it takes only a little bit of doubt to be downright destructive.

Fear can be either your friend or your enemy. As a friend, it's a signal to investigate or ruminate upon something more deeply. Questions that might arise out of fear include: What am I not seeing? What am I missing? How can I be more aligned with my overarching vision? Have I given myself permission to have that outcome?

Both fear and doubt come with corresponding images, hunches, or feelings as to why or why not a project might or might not work, but doubt is an erosion in the foundation of an idea or business. Doubt says, with arms crossed, "This is not going to work. *Prove me wrong.*"

Team leaders or managers are often the carriers of the doubt virus. But getting rid of team members to get rid of doubt is like performing surgery to cure a virus. The paradox of fear and doubt is that they are signals—signals designed to help you refine a shared vision that harnesses your team's creativity, all within the context of a powerful purpose.

The doubt of one frontline employee might not warrant the

expenditure of unnecessary time and energy to address it. If over time, however, you see a trend where your team leaders doubt your initiatives or overall strategy—or if you find that the majority of people in your inner circle aren't buying into it—you're *going* to fail, and there will be a plethora of "extenuating circumstances" and really good reasons for the failure. When it happens, I recommend handling the team's concerns in a professional way, instead of blaming them for mishaps, mistakes, or mishandlings. Perhaps these team members have harmful agreements about each other or you, which takes us to number six.

LOSING STRATEGY #6: PARTICIPATING IN HARMFUL AGREEMENTS

In an organizational setting, a harmful agreement is a covert judgment that two (or more) people share. Harmful agreements can appear as innocuous as a joke or a roll of the eyes, but their ongoing nature makes them far more damaging. Even executives deploy harmful agreements, as do factions of employees, cliques, departments, and even entire companies. Agreements are used to share pain, scapegoat, and avoid responsibility—or be *right* so as to make [insert opposing party] *wrong*. Whether or not an agreement is warranted, know that what we're talking about is an adult version of bullying.

If a group of people in an organization have harmful agreements about you, you're going to have a tough time fulfilling ambitious results with them. It's just a simple, straight up, unavoidable fact. As a CEO, one way to get rid of harmful agreements in your company is through skills training. If done right, this type of training can help people recognize the existence of harmful agreements, define the productive ones, and assess and disassemble the costly, unproductive ones. When they then receive training on *clear* agreements, requests, and promises, because they are already aware of the liabilities of harmful agreements, it's easier to keep the negative ones at bay.

I have personally seen a small group of women coalesce around harmful agreements regarding a male leader. When he became aware of it, I watched him deftly make the individuals who shared the agreements irrelevant within the company. In other words, he figured out how to use them for his needs, then discarded them when his needs were achieved by blocking them from exposure to projects, recognition, and rewards.

That's not to say I don't also see many agreements among men. They, too, have agreements about women, other men, and so on. I think women and men have equal amounts of agreements, but women seem to be better at it, not to mention more insidious. Some people just seem to have a knack for planting little agreement bombs. When their cover gets blown, they'll be the first to blame someone else.

Do not enter into harmful agreements about anyone or anything. And know that if you create harmful agreements about a man and he becomes aware of it, he will unleash the full brunt of his competitive nature toward you. He will be ruthless, systematic, and matter-of-fact about taking you out or putting you at a disadvantage, just to make your life harder.

LOSING STRATEGY #7: BLAMING PEOPLE INSTEAD OF SYSTEMS

Every issue that arises in your company should first be viewed through the prism of a systems failure, and only then should you consider it as a people failure. In the course of doing business, there will be times when mistakes and omissions very clearly look like a situation is the direct result of a personnel problem. I would argue, however, that if you look at it from the thirty-thousand-foot view, the origin of the problem can almost always be traced to a breakdown in hiring, training, procedures, accountability, or management systems. Locate the root cause of the breakdown in the corresponding area and fix it—even while you counsel that "problem" employee or supplier.

If a person has been trained well and according to company procedures, and they've been managed, coached, and held accountable to a set of metrics—and they're *still* presenting a problem—it might also be worth looking at your company's culture and morale. Are you measuring your team's satisfaction and getting feedback? There are software companies such as TINYpulse, Culture Amp, and Officevibe that offer an alternative to the traditional annual engagement survey by using shorter, more frequent check-ins regarding employee satisfaction. This way, you can take the pulse of your company culture on a regular, continuous basis.

If you are implementing things that are measurably proven to make employees happy, while having all these other systems in place, your management mandate can be to always have people fire themselves instead of you doing it. Although I've personally been terrible about implementing this self-firing policy, I recommend learning about it in

Patrick Lencioni's book *The Motive: Why So Many Leaders Abdicate Their Most Important Responsibilities*. In it, Lencioni provides an excellent method for coaching people to either improve or depart from your company. I once heard him lecture, during which he said you must be willing to tell someone that what they are doing is wrong every single day for up to three weeks, accompanied by the statement, "If you don't change this, you're going to get yourself fired."

Every time you have a recurring problem, look first for the system that is broken. Only then counsel the people.

LOSING STRATEGY #8: MARTYRDOM

To call someone a martyr is to say that person thinks she deserves sympathy for being treated badly or for suffering. If you're an entrepreneur and you have the tendency to play the martyr, you need to address it ASAP.

This one I know from observation *and* experience. Several years back, my long-term boyfriend started a new job and was often away on projects. Since I had just hired a CEO to run my company, even though my boyfriend and I weren't married, I decided I wanted to have the experience of playing house (aka being a housewife). By day three, the house was impeccably clean and organized. I was cooking, preparing his meals, packing him lunches, *and I was excited about it*. Then, around day ten, I made him a romantic dinner. When he came home an hour late without letting me know, I let him have it, but not directly. Instead, I subtly slipped into self-pity, and my energy dropped through the floor, even though, all the while, I observed what a cliché I was being. *I am wiser than this*, I thought to myself.

Then, it happened a few more times.

Over time, what ensued between us was a game of push-and-pull, passive-aggressive behaviors, and unnecessary drama. He was out in the world, creating and achieving, and I was sitting in the house unconsciously conjuring up ways to get the intensity I needed.

You see, in the business world, I was used to intensity, accountability, and intrinsically motivated satisfaction for my efforts, and without being able to direct that energy toward a greater goal, I felt unmoored. That's when it dawned on me: while trying to be a good, supportive, service-oriented, encouraging partner, I was living in a state of resentment. (And this happens both ways; for instance, the woman who wants to stay home but has to work.) The experience awakened me to something I learned when my kids were small: living my life for someone else is not a good recipe for living my life.

If you're a female leader, please be aware of this.

Many women—women whom I love, adore, and respect—naturally possess the heart of a servant. While their education and backgrounds vary, what they all have in common is that they *don't* want to lead. Instead, they want to personally support others. These are the women I want helping me, whether they are my nanny, my household manager, or my assistant. If you are *not* this type of female—but *trying* to be—it's time to examine what this pretense is costing you and those around you in terms of vitality, happiness, and income.

If you have the ambition to scale a company, to stay in your leadership function, I recommend you ask for help early, often, and consistently. That means if you're going to have to pay for help—whether that's hiring a therapist, a coach, after-school care, or only someone to pick up your kids from school—you need to do it. To think you're the only one who can be your child's guardian not only puts pressure on yourself, but it's just not true. If you are leading a business, there's no reason for you to sit in line for forty-five minutes to pick up your kids during prime business hours. There are thousands of other ways to connect with your kids other than being "the one" who makes their meals, picks them up, or shops for their groceries.

To do it all, you don't have to be a martyr. Picking and choosing where you want help in your life is not only in your control, but it's a luxury you deserve. Just make sure you have the highest-quality assistance. It will make your life easier...and you, your spouse or significant other, and your children will benefit from your happiness.

LOSING STRATEGY #9: SEDUCTION

Seduction in business, which is the practice of using the energy of attraction as a manipulation tool—rather than fuel for creation—is a game that's played under the radar. I'm not talking necessarily about outright propositioning someone but, rather, using the energies to get one's way. It's like leading someone around by the nose. Even if the victim seems like they like it—you will regret deploying it in the long run.

We're all adults here, right? So let's be honest: sexuality is a force of nature, and whether we are consciously or unconsciously aware of it, it certainly makes itself known in the business world from time to time, sometimes subtly, sometimes overtly.

First, let's talk about the seduction games men play. Both as a professional and as a woman, I've had men test my loyalty to a mission or deal by using the tools of money, authority, and power to try to influence me into ideas or actions that were beneath me. I've seen men attempt to seduce women with exposure, contracts, "help," and favors.

I do business with a considerable number of men in my industry, and we have strong trust and mutual respect. These men have strong balance sheets, high levels of influence, and entrepreneurial genius. I simply love many of them, as platonic friends. As their supplier, I've built a deep level of trust on very candidly telling them when and where I can help them or bluntly telling them I don't have a clue how to help them.

Sometimes male clients, suppliers, or project partners try to get information out of me that I don't want to tell. If that's the case, I simply say, "I don't feel comfortable sharing that right now." Since I don't make them wrong for asking and we have mutual trust and respect, they know I won't lie. They may try to coax me into sharing proprietary information with a joke, but they respect my boundaries and, in turn, know I will respect theirs.

As an IFL, you've likely come across men who deal with you first as a woman, then as a businessperson. If you feel that energy or vibration coming your way, stay awake. I'm not talking about gentlemen who seek to open doors for you, but men who *still see you as the other team,* even though we're well into the twenty-first century. You can always tell the difference because they're the ones who will seduce you by implying, "You're on my team," just to keep you around, *and then fail to add your name or your company's name to the deal.*

When it comes to these types and their sometimes invisible games, the best advice I have for you is this: men can see each other's games from a mile away, so if you have any doubt whether you are being played, ask another man.

As far as the opposite, in business, men don't take women who use seduction as a tool seriously, and they will almost immediately write you off as a serious contender for projects and partnerships if they can seduce you. This goes for being lured into providing confidential information, performing shady business acts, and so forth. If you submit to this type of temptation, the man will be forced to mitigate his risk of exposure to you. You won't know the reason why, but they'll stop returning your phone calls and emails as soon as practically possible. Their conquest is over, and you proved you were not strong enough.

I don't see a lot of seduction originating from female leaders or entrepreneurs because seductresses don't tend to make it to the bargaining table or the boardrooms, the places where actual business is being conducted. Even the women who sell through seduction usually don't last long, due to the fact that—based on promises being made that can't be kept (both personal and business)—the company can't afford to keep them around. The bottom line is, only in Hollywood movies do seductive women achieve positions of real power.

But if a man is attracted to you, don't use it as a tool for manipulation to increase your position or exposure to more business. Be gracious, enjoy feeling attractive, and transmute those energies into providing value to make him look good in business while being squeaky-clean in your interactions. This will help put a stop to the whole practice of using seduction, because it is hindering our moving forward with the global balance we seek.

LOSING STRATEGY #10: PLAYING HOUSE

If you're still reading after all the controversial things I've said so far, then you can handle this next nugget of truth. A lot (certainly not all) of us feminine figures love playing house, and that might include having a partner, having some babies, decorating, entertaining, and other stereotypically feminine things.

The reason I listed "playing house" as a losing strategy is *only* because I've personally cost myself millions over the years, for example, by taking *too long* of a break to settle into a new home (like months) or by getting distracted at the wrong time (like when I should have been strategic planning instead of holiday planning). I actually don't regret playing house, but I wish I had done it more consciously, which I will talk about shortly.

The problem with playing house is that as business owners and boss ladies, in addition to not compartmentalizing each area of our lives, *we also don't report to anyone.* Therefore, we could have a tendency to let our personal lives bleed into professional priorities without limits.

Even though I've said that the ability to create life on your terms is mandatory for IFLs, it's useful to know about the flash points in a woman's career when this urge to swing completely away from business and play house will rear up. It's one thing to fan the flame of romance, for example, but if she gives any one of these events too much oxygen, it can take away her business's momentum.

The following situations are what have caused me to lose ground because I took my eye off the ball for months at a time while my executive team ran my business. Just take my warnings with a grain of salt if they don't apply to you, but here are some significant events to be mindful of:

1. **You're in a new relationship.** This one is for all my single ladies...New relationships, and the blast of oxytocin that comes with them, can cause you to go into a "romance trance." Schedule the romance judiciously, but *know when to turn it off.* You can't be daydreaming about a dinner date when you're in the midst of closing a massive deal. As a healthy adult, you would never let a new relationship get you off track with your children (if you have them), and your business is one of your children.

2. **You move to a new house or are remodeling.** Especially if your company is running fine without you having to be there, your desire to nest can detract from the game. Schedule the remodel and then hire helpers to do all of the packing, unpacking, hanging curtains, and so on. Resist getting caught in the nesting phase for too long, as it will cost you dearly.

3. **Your children change their status.** If you have children, at some point, they will leave for college or move out. Events such as this can distract you from your long-

range vision by knocking you off balance. Therefore, the best antidote is to schedule connecting with your children into your calendar. They're not coming home every day anymore, so don't wait for them to call. Set up a regular time to call or see them, and proactively create some new traditions. Your sadness will subside, and your business will still be there for you.

CHAPTER 9

STAY TRUE TO YOURSELF

"Enough...I quit...stick a fork in me because I am *done* with this sh*t."

I was talking to myself while driving from Austin toward Houston on Interstate 10. I hadn't even bothered to put on makeup, do my hair, or shave my legs. I just threw on a plain blue suit and got in the car to make the two-and-a-half-hour trip to an executive coaching roundtable. It included heavy hitters making breakthrough goals and holding each other accountable—similar to having a board of directors, except *way more intense.* In front of everyone, the female leader of the group called me out on looking like I'd been "rode hard and put up wet," as we say (about horses) in Texas.

Successful leaders all seem to agree that *if you're not growing, you're dying.* I've found this maxim to be accurate, but that day I showed up to the roundtable, I tried pretending it wasn't. From countless books to a wide diversity of workshops, expensive executive peer groups, coaching certifications, and hiring an impressive array of coaches, I had totally immersed myself in personal development. But on that day, I was finished listening to outside information, and her comments didn't faze me.

I wasn't just some run-of-the-mill seminar junkie: I was ultra-rigorous with myself in extracting every possible morsel of value and getting an ROI on my time and financial investment for all the self-development work I did. But suddenly, I'd had the idea that *I'd arrived*, or if not, I wasn't ever going to get where I was headed anyway.

That weekend, I remember sitting by my pool with vodka and Red Bull in hand. I was on the phone talking to a former army officer with whom I had just closed a big deal to co-provide logistics services to the government. My company was set up for the year on revenue, our SOPs were all up-to-date, and my high-performance team was trained and in place. I was now single and had my kids with me every other week.

"I've been thinking—I'm going to take a break for six weeks. I haven't had a break for as long as I can remember," I extolled. I have no idea why I thought six weeks was the magic elixir.

What happened over the next several weeks surprised me. What I quickly discovered was that if you're a leader, there's only so many pillows you can fluff, closets you can organize, and sunbathing you can enjoy before going nuts. I relaxed right into complacency and habituation, and from that place, I felt like I might die from an overdose of predictability.

I realized just how many things the average person in our privileged culture has to pacify herself, and this keeps us in a stultified comfort zone of ease and complacency: computers, social media, takeout, on-demand movies, recliners, video games, machines that do our chores (like how the laundry magically comes out clean after you put it into a machine with soap, as compared to how great-grandma did it).

To gather food, we go to the store, where an exotic assortment of globally sourced items is right at our fingertips. In this culture, there is little that's physically required of us, and I believe technology such as robots and self-driving cars is only going to make it worse.

It now seems like the opportunity to check out of life and still walk around for another twenty, forty, or even sixty years is present like never before in history. So many people seem bored and without a purpose. Many are bitching at the TV or social media, complaining about Democrats, Republicans, big corporations, immigrants, or whoever, whatever, or wherever they choose to place the focus of their ire.

They criticize and judge separation-based, media-manufactured realities rather than putting their energy into real, tangible challenges that bring forth their spirit, creativity, and ingenuity to help humanity, animals, or Mother Earth. I call them "lounge lizards" because they lounge about, putting their attention on whatever crisis the media places before them.

In order to stay true to yourself and not get sucked into the cultural mind control, use your position as an IFL to stay grounded in what's real for you and also to help ground the people within your sphere of influence. Businesses and other workplaces that are led by inspired leaders can be the antidote to a popular culture that divides, labels, and judges.

While billions of dollars are spent every year competing for your focus, as an IFL, you have the power to redirect the conversation. In my company, our people don't tend to go home and engage in drama because what they have going on during the day is intense enough (and way more interesting). I love hearing from them that they don't just see the business as "a job to go to," but rather a place to grow and have fun.

When you have to solve issues, serve people, and help a team, it causes you to wake up. It's there, in that space, that things are more vivid and more real than on reality TV or the so-called news. A good leader will even manufacture worthy causes for people to follow and design celebration systems around achieving the results. People have to put food on the table by participating in business and the economy in one way or another. So you might as well make it a game.

I have people on my team past retirement age who have more fun than they would if they were kicking back in their recliner. I have young, inexperienced people who, although they lack a degree or they came from an unrelated industry, are getting to do things they never thought they'd be doing. I take a risk on them because when we push people out of their comfort zones, they go into the *unknown*—and that's where the alchemy happens in business.

When we go into the unknown, we go into a state of play, which is where we are most true to our real nature. The facilitator of that roundtable, who called me out on how I showed up to the meeting in Houston, wasn't just calling me out on my appearance. She was holding me accountable for *not being true to myself*. I could have fallen down the rabbit hole of self-pity, and I did, in fact, take an unscheduled sabbatical the next week. But her stand for my being true to myself, in comparison to how I felt trying to be someone I'm not, had me choose to get back in the game.

YOU ALWAYS HAVE A CHOICE

Children. Relationship issues. Sick or aging parents. Following your spouse to another job...in another city. Your refusal to outsource chores, fear of delegating, or inability to surrender control. When it comes to running a business, there are countless deterrents to getting the job done—and when they surface, even more reasons to want to quit.

Just remember that the choice is always yours. Even though it's a very significant event to leave a company that you own, it can be done if you find that continuing down that path is no longer something you can authentically enjoy. The choices you have are (1) you can sell your company, (2) you can give away your company, or (3) you can shut down your company.

Unexpected occurrences are going to happen in life, each of which has the potential to knock you off your game. This may occur anywhere from several times a year to more than once in a single day. Should this happen to you, hopefully, it's long after your business has taken on a life of its own. That way, you can "pretend quit" and keep it to yourself while you wait for the mood to pass. *The point is, don't use excuses for not being true yourself.*

With that said, let's take a little pause for self-examination. This exercise is more important than you might think, which is why I recommend it to my fellow feminine entrepreneurs who are starting out. Why is it so important? Because it harkens back to business as your spiritual path.

Try taking out a notebook or a piece of paper and writing down everything that is thwarting your business ambitions or causing them to falter. For example, you're concerned about what people think when you go on business trips and leave your kids with your husband, relative, or nanny. Or you can't seem to find time to exercise and get your work done, so you've become completely sedentary.

Chances are more than likely some of these need addressing—because you can count on your business to amplify those areas of your life that aren't working. These are those dimly lit corners where cobwebs and dust bunnies have been subtly accumulating, and although they drive you batsh*t crazy, you've quietly learned to tolerate them. Over time, you feel more like you have sacrificed who you really are. The culprit could be outside factors, lack of self-care, no role models, or just the need for a mental or physical tune-up.

All of this is to say—instead of choosing to quit—look at taking care of yourself as an investment that could include things like massage therapy, travel, a home gym, health coaching, business coaching, couples counseling, chiropractic care, a cleaning crew for your house—basically any arena of your life that could use improvement. The idea is that you want to level up all deficient areas so as to maximize your performance—because high performance leads to breakthroughs. To do that, sometimes you need to ask for help.

BE COMFORTABLE ASKING FOR HELP

"I don't have a condition..."

I had looked in the yellow pages for an adult-sitter service. (You know, those agencies that send help to elderly people who can't walk or drive?)

"Do you have someone you could send today?" I had asked in my best sales voice.

The sweet woman on the phone assured me they had sitters ready to go to work today; they just needed to get some information first:

"Who is this for, and what is his or her condition?"

"It's for me," I said.

Five minutes before, I'd nearly fainted—not because blood was running down the side of my son's head, but because I was the one who made him bleed.

As a rambunctious two-year-old, he was playing rough around his five-month-old sister and went too far. She cried loudly. Out of delirious exhaustion, I swatted the top of his head with the piece of laundry I was folding at the time. It wasn't a hard hit, but had the desired effect—he stopped acting so physical in her vicinity. But the piece of laundry I was folding at the time was a baby jacket with a metal zipper. While he went back to playing without a whimper, I could have punched myself at the sight of his blood. (He healed quickly, but that spot on his head was flaky and dry for years afterward. He often had to scratch it, a constant reminder of my abusive action.)

A couple of weeks before, my husband and I had moved our entire ecosystem, including our one-year-old business, to another city.

In the midst of unpacking, taking care of business, breast-feeding twins, and handling the housework, I'd resisted calling a nanny service because professional nannies expect to handle children instead of heavy housework, and I didn't want to watch someone play with my kids while I cleaned, cooked, ran errands, and organized. I also didn't want a house-cleaning service because they typically don't do laundry, disinfect toys, change litter boxes, and a bunch of other things I wanted help with.

So I called an adult daycare company and asked for someone to help me with the same things they'd help a bedridden adult with: laundry, cooking, shopping, and cleaning. They only helped with childcare when I made business calls.

This began a new era in both my professional and personal life. That era continues to this day, and it involves me asking for help *before*, *during*, and *after* I think I might need it. Because if I don't ask for help when I need it, I will let someone down. That someone might be myself, my family, my clients, or my employees.

It took a couple of personal assistants to pull off a successful first year of operations, and I hired them without worrying about the cost, even though it seemed outrageously expensive at the time. Because of my not wanting to put stress into my kids (like the zipper on my son's head), having enough support was the only option. The freedom these assistants gave me to focus on what I needed to accomplish cemented the role's importance, so from then on, I had assistants for the next several years.

Regardless of whether you have outside assistants, it's also important to demand help inside your household. Explain the context to your loved ones that, as a leader, in your unique role, you could use their support, and outline what that entails in the form of a written weekly checklist. Explain to your daughters and sons that leadership is something that may take some of your attention from them when you are together, but explain to them how you are helping create jobs and feed more families and how by being part of your family, they are helping you serve other families.

So ask yourself: What do you do when you're faced with more tasks than you think you can handle? Do you try to do it all anyway? Do you get anxious and stressed? Do you complain and punish the people around you? Do you become aloof and distant? Or do you freeze up and procrastinate?

"I've got so much to do. I'm overwhelmed. I'm buried. I'm covered up with work. I have no idea how I'll get all this done." When you say these things, your body makes a certain set of chemicals. Do you feel like your true, best self when this happens? I hope not, or else you might be addicted to the chemicals of stress. When stress and overwhelm become habitual, this can lead us to behaviors, decisions, and a lifestyle that lacks a certain, shall we say, *sobriety*.

If you don't ask for clear and direct help with what you need, you'll never experience being true to your authentic self as your business grows and you become more successful (if you can even reach success without that kind of help).

Because when a person gets used to feeling overwhelmed as her natural state, she'll never quite feel like she's "arrived." And she certainly won't experience the awesome sensation of loving her life and having it all.

If having it all—abundance, relaxation, contribution to others, happiness, health, a great family, friends, and connection to yourself, others, and the divine—sounds like something you can handle, but you're still having trouble asking for help, consider the following:

> When you hire someone to help you, you are feeding that person's family in addition to them helping you feed your own. When you set someone up for success in giving you exactly what you need, you open your heart and give someone a chance to be of service.

You also get to learn to trust. You let go of everything having to be perfect. Even if you have to replace that person a few times, you'll learn something new each time about how to hire the right person, how to give clear instructions and feedback, and how to give yourself permission to receive the support.

Consider any areas in your life where you're sacrificing

some aspect of yourself as a possible area to upgrade your support system.

If anxious thoughts arise for you as a result of having a business and also having roles outside the business, rest assured, you *can* have both. It's not one or the other. Of course, your business is like having a dependent, so you will have to do whatever it takes regardless of whether you have enough help at any given time.

WHAT ARE FRIENDS FOR?

The author and motivational speaker Jim Rohn has been famously quoted as saying, "We are the average of the five people we spend the most time with." No one can deny the great life pleasure that is connecting with your best friends, laughing all night, and feeling relaxed enough to let your realness shine. For me, however, it just so happens that many of my very best friends have come as a result of doing business.

I suspect as you grow your company, you're going to attract into your life people with whom you will deeply connect, all while exchanging elevated ideas, information, useful feedback, vitality, and belief in each other's vision and potential. It's been my experience that by staying connected with a degree of regularity to other successful visionaries and entrepreneurs, they can help you stay on top of your game, not to mention help you avoid being sucked into the day-to-day minutiae.

When we have our heads down as such, sometimes we get stuck in limited or myopic thinking, especially in the face of prolonged business challenges. If you don't have these human mirrors, you may lose connection with your company's long-range goals and/or the initial ambition that drove you to take up the mantle of entrepreneurship to begin with. Bottom line—*stay connected to other people who are living in the unknown along with you.*

If you aren't actively scheduling conversations with these kindred spirits into your calendar, you run the risk of losing your connection to that very pure, high-frequency state—the same one that drove you to be an entrepreneur in the first place. From experience, I can tell you that losing that connection can be very costly in terms of your vitality and financial success. These fellow leaders and their reflections serve as sounding boards, and if I go for more than a few weeks without interacting with them, I tend to lose sight of the big picture.

As an example, I once met with a powerful friend for a coffee, during which he convinced me to not only increase my rates by 250 percent, he also talked me into only working for an equity stake in the companies where I consulted. He recognized that potential in me—*and reflected it back to me*—before I even saw it in myself. I have thousands of examples like this. What they each have in common is that sometimes you're the mirror, and sometimes you're the reflection.

This is why studies have shown that the number one determinant as to whether or not we are overweight is our circle of friends. I believe the same can be said for what determines whether we make other choices that are good for us.

HATERS AND LOVERS

In some ways, being the boss can be quite a lonely road, especially if you live in a small to medium-sized town. If you have a particular way of living your life or a visionary way of doing business that's counter to the way "things have always been done," you'll find some people alienating themselves from you. If you find yourself asking why, the answer is more than likely that they don't know what to make of you, not to mention they probably aren't used to that type of boldness from a woman.

It's not uncommon to regularly hear vile comments about top female public figures. Compared to masculine public figures, even for someone you don't necessarily agree with, the slurs are exceptionally cutting. Then there are always those folks who automatically assume you're driving a car your husband bought you or make remarks about how you must be a drug dealer to afford the house you live in.

The reason why I mention these facts of life is because I want you to be aware of these ignorant, jealous, uninformed, or unhappy people so you are prepared when presented with their judgments and projections. Why? Because as an IFL, when you rise, you're going to find yourself unwittingly confronted by one or more of these opinions. The bad news is it comes with the territory. The good news is it means you're kicking ass.

The bottom line—ignore the haters or dissenters. Instead, keep embodying your divine feminine energy, be in service, and be a living example to others that they, too, can live an inspired life dictated by their internal compass.

As I mentioned earlier, when my kids were growing up in our suburban town, several women made mean comments, questioning my loyalty to my kids versus my involvement in my career. I didn't bother trying to get approval from them or making them feel bad for judging. Why would I bother competing with them? They made a choice, but that wasn't my choice. Of course, I would never say this directly to them, and yet at the same time, they felt compelled to comment on my status as a professional, the business attire I was sometimes still wearing at after-school practices and games, or the monetary donations I made to baked-goods sales instead of actually baking the goods.

Perhaps one of the hardest things I had to do was surrender the notion that on a moment-to-moment basis, I was the best person to control how my children were raised. While it was clear I was having the greatest influence upon them, I learned that I didn't have to be a helicopter mom.

Now, when it comes to romantic relationships, I'll be the first to admit I'm no expert. I love connection with men and adore them, but as far as having a great marriage as an IFL, I tried it once, and it didn't work. Probably because we were married at twenty-two and I felt like I was becoming a new person every six months or so.

When we started the company, I assumed the role of CEO from my masculine energy, having no idea that there would be a cost to embodying that energy for years to come. Since then, I've definitely learned how to use my business to dial up my feminine energy instead of making it disappear, and this has positively affected my relationships.

I once met a famous female cognitive-behavioral scientist who said, "Everyone at work is a man." In a way, I see her point. However, with the thoughts contained in this book, current trends, and your success as an Inspired Feminine Leader, I trust a societal evolution is occurring that provides women with the option of being feminine *and* a top leader at work. An awakening to this seems to be happening, albeit slowly.

LEAVE THE BOARDROOM OUT OF THE BEDROOM

"Do you ever turn it off?"

"You think too much."

"I don't like the way you said that."

"I feel criticized right now."

As a successful CEO, have you ever been told any of these things by a man and not understood why on earth he was saying it? If so, don't beat yourself up. It's probably a matter of not compartmentalizing, like they know how to do very well.

In spite of your being an IFL, you might endure short periods of having to come from your masculine energy at work—especially during times of danger to the organization. To counteract that energy, most female leaders I know would *love* to come home and be treated like a woman. Besides those who enjoy fulfilling the masculine role in relationships (whether with another woman or man), the majority of my friends tell me they want to be able to "let go" around a strong, supportive partner who grounds them. In my experience, that is simply not going to happen if she comes home and talks (and acts) like a CEO every day.

Theoretically, if a woman is a leader at work and brings it to the kitchen table, a really smart, intuitive, and confident man would indeed know how to separate the boss from the babe. But that's setting the bar extremely high for a masculine figure, just like the bar is high for feminine figures at the top of companies. In the end, the challenges posed to men on this front have caused many of my female leader friends, against their preferences, to end up alone.

Think of it as a "glass cliff" for men: you really want them to rise up, but they eventually opt out (either energetically or literally) because you never really organize around their unique qualities in a strong role. Once you get used to that angular, linear, focused way of problem-solving and dominating in the name of more exceptional results, if you continue to linger in a masculine state at home and elsewhere, you will actually come across as being competitive with your man.

According to one of my girlfriends, a German relationship coach, many men in the United States have revealed to her that they long for a deep connection with a feminine woman because women who block or suppress their feminine energies all day at work tend to create a wall within themselves. This tendency toward the suppression of her femininity in order to stay focused, stay competitive, and maintain control prevents her from being playful or vulnerable at home.

This is why, at the end of the day, I think it's imperative for any feminine entrepreneur to have rituals to bring her back into her true, natural self (that is, if she has a tendency to turn this off during the day). For a woman who is raising kids as a single mom, this is even more difficult because when she gets home, she has to play mom *and* dad; hence, having some assistance helps tremendously.

One way I've kept the boardroom out of the bedroom, so to speak, would happen when I was in a conversation with my man and heard myself speaking to him as if he were one of my employees. (This was most likely to happen right after work.) I would say, "Apparently, I'm still on the business channel." Of course, he could already feel it. But sometimes you just need to unwind before you can get there.

If this whole thing reeks of an unfair double standard for us, it's also a double standard for the man in your life to expect him to be both receptive and strong for you. So with that, my advice: if you want a straight man to make you feel like a woman, you're going to have to take off the suit of armor. Speaking of...

TAKE OFF YOUR SUIT OF ARMOR

The same year my company broke a bunch of records and added several business units, I was asked to facilitate a conference in Europe. Due to some intense business challenges in my company, I'd been under pressure for some time, so I showed up at the conference in a wound-up state. There was a certain hardness to my thinking, my talk, and even my walk.

It wasn't until I was enveloped in the energy of hundreds of women and feminine leaders that I was awakened to the fact that I was regularly relying on my masculine energy to be effective. How could I teach feminine leadership if I'd become that far out of balance? That epiphany caused me to decide that I was going to do something I'd never seen done before. This was when I decided to lead my companies from my feminine energy at least 80 percent of the time, *even in times of great challenge.*

Leading from my feminine side was at first strange and unfamiliar, and that continues to this day. Because it required me to yield more, I began building consensus in a different way. Whereas you might initially think this was empowering, believe it or not, I felt like I was invisible and that I wasn't being heard. As I overcame the habit of relying on the power of my role in the hierarchy and refined the habit of clearly stating what I wanted and yielding to how the team got it accomplished, my lifestyle changed from one of constant vigilance to one of relaxation.

Besides leading teams without wearing armor, it also works at home. After a tough day at work, we may accidentally talk to our children in an aggressive, unconscious manner. Regrettably for the kids, they just happen to be on the receiving end of a day's (or sometimes weeks' or months') worth of built-up, intense energy. For this reason, on those days, I encourage you to figure out a way to decompress and clear your energy *before* getting it all over your family. It could be taking a walk, processing the day with a call to your friend on your way home from work, exercising, listening to classical music, or whatever else brings you tranquility and chillaxes your soul.

The state of tranquility you bring home at the end of the day turns into the trait of your household, and eventually, your life. That trait, and the artful way you cultivate it over time, is the real return on the investment of being an Inspired Feminine Leader. This cultivation becomes "the game within the game" and is the most rewarding endeavor I've ever undertaken.

CONCLUSION

INSPIRED FEMININE LEADERS AS AGENTS OF CHANGE

We are not our genders.

We are not our stories.

We are not our names, our sexual orientations, or our skin colors.

We are not our cultures.

We are individual aspects of a collective consciousness manifested in a physical, three-dimensional reality. Throughout history, at different times, in different parts of the world, spoken through different voices, said in different ways—from Christ to Krishna to Buddha to Abraham to Muhammad, and beyond—the greatest masters, teachers, sages, saints, and mystics have alluded to, or spoke of, this reality as a dream from which to awaken.

What would be possible if all the leaders of the world became empowered and awakened from this separation-based dream all at once? And what would happen if their collaborations were inclusive of the invaluable qualities of both masculine and feminine figures instead of gender-based tribalism? When the collective "she" accepts her true calling as a leader, and merges her creative energy with the collective masculine, while the masculine gets curious about building systems that support feminine energy, the world as we know it will transform.

I believe that if we could achieve this level of unity consciousness, balanced leadership would end needless violence, child abuse, human trafficking, homelessness, starvation, addiction epidemics, and extraordinarily high incarceration rates. I think we'll take the mixed bag of the progress we've made as humans and get wildly more creative about how we can solve the world's biggest remaining problems *and* earn a profit.

We would be more apt to take care of one another, and we would recognize that there is enough—enough food, enough water, enough money, enough support, enough resources, enough technology, enough compassion, and enough love. This is the resonant truth of the heart of our being.

The time to shift outcomes and break free from past patterns and reactions is upon us. Since it's the woman's responsibility to birth the child, perhaps it's time for us to become responsible for the birth of humanity's new epoch. In this moment of ever-expanding awareness, we need courageous, heart-based Inspired Feminine Leadership talent to lead us from gestation to manifestation. We can help humanity to uncover the genius of our combined masculine/feminine perspectives and create a path to everyone thriving. Together, we can eventually remove the overuse of gender labels and victimhood stories while honoring the roles we came here to play. If we can achieve heart-centered leadership on earth, humanity will begin to shift.

At the *microcosm* of business leadership, the balance of masculine and feminine energies can be utilized to create brilliant companies with compelling missions. These companies will not only generate revenues and returns but provide sufficient incomes and advancement for employees—*in addition* to serving and uplifting the communities in which they operate.

On the *macrocosm* of global leadership, this balanced approach to problem-solving could generate new levels of prosperity and opportunities across the planet, while creating genuine, lasting peace that begins in our families and spreads out across borders. If you believe the greater part of your humanity exists in your divinity, and you believe in divinity's power to create, then you are more powerful than you could ever imagine.

In business ownership, you get to create your life with more freedom of almost every kind. Because I have witnessed this firsthand, my dream is that vast numbers of women learn how to build businesses around the simple truth of being themselves while succeeding at the way the game is played.

WHAT ARE YOU WAITING FOR?

Since my businesses essentially now run themselves, the

next phase of my life's mission (and the purpose of this book) is to ultimately be a contributor to world peace. By encouraging leaders such as yourself to step away from the glass cliff, we will make the shift.

While the case for the unification of divine masculine and feminine energies is evident to most people, what isn't so obvious is that multinational businesses can be the pivotal force in making global peace and balance happen more effectively and efficiently.

When we return to the wholeness that is available—within the individual, our businesses, our governments, and our foreign policies—a new model of leadership will emerge.

So what are you waiting for?

The world is waiting for you.

ACKNOWLEDGMENTS

My sincerest thanks to my parents, who, in raising me in a decidedly masculine way, provided me with the ability to deftly traverse the gender gap in business leadership—and survive to tell about it. With the teachers and mentors who have shown up throughout my life, I've been able to recross this great divide and reclaim my femininity in order to share my learnings with women around the world. Thanks to my mentor Martin Sage for pointing out the divide and for recognizing so many years ago that I had this book in me. To Barbara Jansen, a superb coach who spent countless hours interviewing me and inspiring me to write. No other human has kicked my butt with such style and grace. Michael Otto, thank you for grounding me and having the curiosity to sit through so many hours of my verbal processing. Tim Shields, thank you for helping me get through the birth of this version of the book, and for taking me on the most hilarious and healing quarantine adventure I could have imagined.

Sincerest of gratitude to my three children, who, over the years, have learned to put up with me and somehow managed to thrive on this intense journey. When you have three beautiful, impressionable beings absorbing and observing everything you do and say, it forces you to walk the talk—and to be a better human in the process. You have been my inspiration.

Lastly, I thank the extraordinary, loving team at Team Housing Solutions, the worldwide corporate housing company we built together using the principles and distinctions mentioned in this book. We've been cut and polished like diamonds in a way that wouldn't have occurred had we not come together in such a volatile, complex business environment with the conscious intention of being high performance.

These are the people, especially my "female VP," aka *Mom*, who helped me get it right (when I did get it right) and loved me unconditionally through the process.

ABOUT THE AUTHOR

MANDY CAVANAUGH'S passion for leadership, entrepreneurship, and helping people thrive has fueled her roles as CEO, consultant, facilitator, and workshop leader. As an active serial entrepreneur, Mandy's businesses have included a global accommodations-service company, a manufacturing plant, a land development company, commercial and residential real estate, a resort and wedding venue, a seminar company, and a turnaround consultancy. Her turnaround business included clients in the global security, publishing, commercial construction, industrial process, and healthcare industries.

Mandy credits her ability to succeed in highly competitive environments to activating each of her team member's capacity to connect to his or her best future self. She holds certifications in High-Performance Leadership Coaching and Conscious Language and Outcome Facilitation. She's conducted seminars on breakthrough performance, authentic success, wealth wisdom for women, the language of creation, imagination activation, conflict resolution, CEO-ship for startups, customer service, clear agreements, building teams, and sales. She resides in Texas and has three grown children.

NOTES

INTRODUCTION

1   Saul Mcleod, "Maslow's Hierarchy of Needs," *Simply Psychology*, last modified March 20, 2020, https://www.simplypsychology.org/maslow.html.

2   Alex Fradera., "There Are a Lot of Myths and Misconceptions about Abraham Maslow and Self-Actualization—A New Paper Puts the Record Straight," *Research Digest*, May 17, 2018, https://digest.bps.org.uk/2018/05/17/there-are-a-lot-of-myths-and-misconceptions-about-abraham-maslow-and-self-actualisation-a-new-paper-puts-the-record-straight/.

3   Tim Kaiser, Marco Del Giudice, and Tom Booth, "Global Sex Differences in Personality: Replication with an Open Online Dataset," *Journal of Personality* 88, no. 3 (July 15, 2019), https://doi.org/10.1111/jopy.12500.

4   Stephan Spencer, "111: Finding Your Relationship Style and a Love That Lasts," September 5, 2017, in *Get Your Life Optimized*, podcast, 42:53, https://www.getyourselfoptimized.com/finding-relationship-style-love-lasts-dr-pat-allen/.

CHAPTER 1

5   "Women in the Workplace 2019," McKinsey & Company, September 1, 2015, https://www.mckinsey.com/business-functions/organization/our-insights/women-in-the-workplace.

6   Michelle K. Ryan and S. Alexander Haslam, "The Glass Cliff: Evidence That Women Are Over-Represented in Precarious Leadership Positions," *British Journal of Management* 16, no. 2 (February 9, 2005): 81–90.

7   Barney Glaser and Anslem Strauss, *The Discovery of Grounded Theory* (Chicago: Aldine, 1967); J. Hall, "We Don't Want to Be the Boss," *Sunday Telegraph*, June 19, 2005; Patricia Sellers and Jenny Mero, "Power: Do Women Really Want It? That's the Surprising Question More of Them Are Asking When They Ponder Top Jobs in Business, Academia, and Government," *Fortune Magazine*, October 13, 2003, https://money.cnn.com/magazines/fortune/fortune_archive/2003/10/13/350932/index.htm; Claudia Wallis, "The Case for Staying Home: Why More Young Moms Are Opting Out of the Rat Race," *Time*, March 22, 2004, 22, 52–58.

8   Lawrence H. Summers, "Remarks at NBER Conference on Diversifying the Science and Engineering Workforce," Harvard University, January 14, 2005, https://www.harvard.edu/president/speech/2005/remarks-nber-conference-on-diversifying-science-engineering-workforce.

9   Anna Fels, "Do Women Lack Ambition?" *Harvard Business Review*, April 2004, 82, 50–60.

10   Nic Paton, "Women Are Less Ambitious than Men: and Men Are to Blame," *Management Issues*, November 23, 2006, https://www.management-issues.com/news/3790/women-are-less-ambitious---and-men-are-to-blame/.

11   Sylvia Ann Hewlett and Carolyn Buck Luce, "Off-Ramps and On-Ramps: Keeping Talented Women on the Road to Success," *Harvard Business Review*, March 2005, 1–10.

12   Hewlett and Luce, "Off-Ramps."

13   Hewlett and Luce, "Off-Ramps."

14   Pamela Stone and Meg Lovejoy, "Fast-Track Women and the 'Choice' to Stay Home," *Annals of the American Academy of Political and Social Science* 596 (November 2004): 62–83; Linda K. Stroh, Jeanne M. Brett, and Anne H. Reilly, "Family Structure, Glass Ceiling, and Traditional Explanations for the Differential Rate of Turnover of Female and Male Managers," *Journal of Vocational Behavior* 49, no. 1 (August 1996): 99–118.

15   Ryan and Haslam, "The Glass Cliff," 81–90; James R. Meindl, Sanford B. Ehrlich, and Janet M. Dukerich, "The Romance of Leadership," *Administrative Science Quarterly* 30, no. 1 (March 1985): 78–102.

16   Michelle K. Ryan, S. Alexander Haslam, Mette D. Hersby, Clara Kulich, and Cate Atkins, "Opting Out or Pushed off the Edge? The Glass Cliff and the Precariousness of Women's Leadership Positions," *Social and Personality Psychology Compass* 1, no. 1 (November 2007): 266–279, https://doi.org/10.1111/j.1751-9004.2007.00007.x.

17   Debra L. Nelson, and James C. Quick, "Professional Women: Are Distress and Disease Inevitable?" *Academy of Management Review* 10, no. 2 (April 1985): 206–218, https://doi.org/10.2307/257963.

18   Debra L. Nelson, James Campbell Quick, and Michael A. Hitt, "Men and Women of the Personnel Profession: Some Differences and Similarities in Their Stress," *Stress Medicine* 5, no. 3 (July/September 1989): 145–152, https://doi.org/10.1002/smi.2460050304.

19 Rosalind C. Barnett and Grace K. Baruch, "Women's Involvement in Multiple Roles and Psychological Distress," *Journal of Personality and Social Psychology* 49, no. 1 (1985): 135–145, https://doi.org/10.1037/0022-3514.49.1.135.

20 Karen Pugliesi, "The Consequences of Emotional Labor: Effects on Work Stress, Job Satisfaction, and Well-Being," *Motivation and Emotion* 23 (June 1999): 125–154.

21 Nelson, Quick, and Hitt, "Men and Women of the Personnel Profession," 145–152

22 Stephen J. Motowidlo, John S. Packard, and Michael R. Manning, "Occupational Stress: Its Causes and Consequences for Job Performance," *Journal of Applied Psychology* 71, no. 4 (December 1986): 616–629, https://doi.org/10.1037/0021-9010.71.4.618.

23 Cary L. Cooper and Stephen Williams, *Creating Healthy Work Organisations* (Chichester, UK: John Wiley & Sons, 1994).

24 Paul E. Spector, Daniel J. Dwyer, and Steve M. Jex, "Relation of Job Stressors to Affective, Health, and Performance Outcomes: A Comparison of Multiple Data Sources," *Journal of Applied Psychology* 73, no. 1 (1988): 11–19, https://doi.org/10.1037/0021-9010.73.1.11.

25 Claude M. Steele and Joshua Aronson, "Stereotype Threat and the Intellectual Test Performance of African Americans," *Journal of Personality and Social Psychology* 69, no. 5 (1995): 797–811, https://doi.org/10.1037/0022-3514.69.5.797.

26 S. Alexander Haslam, Jolanda Jetten, Anne O'Brien, and Elissa Jacobs, "Social Identity, Social Influence, and Reactions to Potentially Stressful Tasks: Support for the Self-Categorization Model of Stress," *Stress and Health* 20, no. 1 (February 2004): 3–9, https://doi.org/10.1002/smi.995.

27 Daan Van Knippenberg, "Work Motivation and Performance: A Social Identity Perspective," *Applied Psychology: An International Review* 49, no. 3 (December 2001): 357–371, https://doi.org/10.1111/1464-0597.00020.

28 Tom R. Tyler and Steven L. Blader, "Identity and Cooperative Behavior In Groups," *Group Processes and Intergroup Relations* 4 (July 1, 2001): 207–226, https://doi.org/10.1177/1368430 201004003003.

29 S. Alexander Haslam, Michelle K. Ryan, Tom Postmes, Russell Spears, Jolanda Jetten, and Paul Webley, "Sticking to Our Guns: Social Identity as a Basis for the Maintenance of Commitment to Faltering Organizational Projects," *Journal of Organizational Behaviour* 27, no. 5 (June 21, 2006): 607–628, https://doi.org/10.1002/job.370.

30 Ryan et al., "Opting Out or Pushed off the Edge?" 266–279.

31 Eilene Zimmerman, "Only 2% of Women-Owned Businesses Break the $1 Million Mark—Here's How to Be One of Them," *Forbes*, April 1, 2015, https://www.forbes.com/sites/eilenezimmerman/2015/04/01/only-2-of-women-owned-businesses-break-the-1-million-mark-heres-how-to-be-one-of-them/#7a7ff6ac27a6.

32   Carolyn Turner, "A Balance of Both Masculine and Feminine Strengths: The Bottom-Line Benefit." *Forbes*, May 7, 2012, https://www.forbes.com/sites/womensmedia/2012/05/07/a-balance-of-both-masculine-and-feminine-strengths-the-bottom-line-benefit/#23714ecf79e7.

33   Victor W. Hwang, "Are Feminine Leadership Traits the Future of Business?" *Forbes*, August 30, 2014, https://www.forbes.com/sites/victorhwang/2014/08/30/are-feminine-leadership-traits-the-future-of-business/#9f1f63f598e5.

34   "Women Pioneered Computer Programming. Then Men Took Their Industry Over. How 'Computer Girls' Gave Way to Tech Bros," *Timeline*, May 16, 2017, https://timeline.com/women-pioneered-computer-programming-then-men-took-their-industry-over-c2959b822523.

35   "Women in the Workplace 2019."

CHAPTER 2

36   Todd M. Thrash and Andrew J. Elliot, "Inspiration as a Psychological Construct," *Journal of Personality and Social Psychology* 84, no. 4 (May 2003): 871–889, https://doi.org/10.1037/0022-3514.84.4.871.

37   Scott Barry Kaufman, "Why Inspiration Matters," *Harvard Business Review*, November 8, 2011, https://hbr.org/2011/11/why-inspiration-matters#:~:text=Inspiration%20awakens%20us%20to%20new,because%20of%20its%20elusive%20nature.

38   Marina Milyavskaya, Iana Ianakieva, Emily Foxen-Craft, Agnes Colantuoni, and Richard Koestner, "Inspired to Get There: The Effects of Trait and Goal Inspiration on Goal Progress," *Personality and Individual Differences* 52, no. 1 (January 2012): 56–60, https://doi.org/10.1016/j.paid.2011.08.031.

39   Joe Dispenza, *Becoming Supernatural: How Common People Are Doing the Uncommon*, 2nd ed. (Carlsbad, CA: Hay House, 2019), 93–96.

40   Dr. Ananya Mandal, "What Is the Thalamus?" News Medical Lifesciences, February 27, 2019, https://www.news-medical.net/health/What-is-the-Thalamus.aspx.

41   Janice Friedman, "The Ancient Egyptians Knew How to Unleash the Power of the Pineal Gland," Ancient Code, accessed September 23, 2020, https://www.ancient-code.com/ancient-egyptians-knew-unleash-power-pineal-gland/.

42   Robert M. Sargis, "An Overview of the Pineal Gland: Maintaining Circadian Rhythm," Endocrineweb, last modified on June 10, 2014, https://www.endocrineweb.com/endocrinology/overview-pineal-gland.

43   Joe Dispenza, *Becoming Supernatural*, 275–279.

44   Joseph Jaworski, *Synchronicity: The Inner Path of Leadership* (San Francisco, CA: Berrett-Koehler, 1996).

CHAPTER 3

45 "The Brain-Gut Connection," Johns Hopkins, accessed June 4, 2019, https://www. hopkinsmedicine.org/health/wellness-and-prevention/the-brain-gut-connection.

46 "Do Economic or Industry Factors Affect Business Survival?" Small Business Office of Advocacy, June 2012, https://www.sba.gov/sites/default/files/Business-Survival.pdf.

47 "Know Your Brain: Amygdala," Neuroscientifically Challenged, June 24, 2014, https://www. neuroscientificallychallenged.com/blog/know-your-brain-amygdala.

CHAPTER 4

48 Scott Barry Kaufman, "Why Inspiration Matters," *Harvard Business Review*, November 8, 2011, https://hbr.org/2011/11/why-inspiration-matters#:~:text=Inspiration%20awakens%20 us%20to%20new,because%20of%20its%20elusive%20nature.

CHAPTER 5

49 Robert Taibbi, "Wire Together Fire Together: Time to Make New Connections?" *Psychology Today*, June 2, 2013, https://www.psychologytoday.com/us/blog/fixing-families/201306/ wire-together-fire-together-time-make-new-connections.

50 Susanne Bruckmüller and Nyla R. Branscombe, "The Glass Cliff: When and Why Women Are Selected as Leaders in Crisis Contexts," *British Journal of Social Psychology* 49, no. 3 (August 18, 2009), https://doi.org/10.1348/014466609X466594.

51 Polly Young-Eisendrath and Terence Dawson, *The Cambridge Companion to Jung* (Cambridge, MA: Cambridge University Press, 1997).

52 Carl G. Jung, *Collected Works of C.G. Jung*, 2nd ed., vol. 9, pt. 2 (Princeton, NJ: Princeton University Press, 2014); Carl G. Jung, *Aion: Researches into the Phenomenology of the Self*, 2nd ed. (Princeton, NJ: Princeton University Press, 1979).

CHAPTER 6

53 Michael Lenneville, "Is a Bad Mood Contagious?" *Scientific American*, July 1, 2012, https:// www.scientificamerican.com/article/is-a-bad-mood-contagious.

CHAPTER 7

54 Jackson J. Spielvogel, *Western Civilization: Volume B: 1300–1815*, 10th ed. (Boston, MA: Cengage Learning, 2017), 549.

Made in the USA
Monee, IL
11 February 2022

91129143R00142